# Ancestral Healing

## Made Easy

**Also in the *Made Easy* series**

*The Akashic Records*

*Animal Communication*

*Astrology*

*Chakras*

*Connecting with the Angels*

*Connecting with the Fairies*

*Crystals*

*Discovering Your Past Lives*

*Energy Healing*

*Feng Shui*

*Goddess Wisdom*

*Lucid Dreaming*

*Meditation*

*Mediumship*

*Mindfulness*

*NLP*

*Numerology*

*Qabalah*

*Reiki*

*Self-Hypnosis*

*Shamanism*

*Tantra*

*The Tarot*

# Ancestral Healing Made Easy

## How to Resolve Ancestral Patterns and Honour Your Family History

Natalia and Terry O'Sullivan

HAY HOUSE
Carlsbad, California • New York City
London • Sydney • New Delhi

**Published in the United Kingdom by:**
Hay House UK Ltd, The Sixth Floor, Watson House,
54 Baker Street, London W1U 7BU
Tel: +44 (0)20 3927 7290; Fax: +44 (0)20 3927 7291; www.hayhouse.co.uk

**Published in the United States of America by:**
Hay House Inc., PO Box 5100, Carlsbad, CA 92018-5100
Tel: (1) 760 431 7695 or (800) 654 5126
Fax: (1) 760 431 6948 or (800) 650 5115; www.hayhouse.com

**Published in Australia by:**
Hay House Australia Pty Ltd, 18/36 Ralph St, Alexandria NSW 2015
Tel: (61) 2 9669 4299; Fax: (61) 2 9669 4144; www.hayhouse.com.au

**Published in India by:**
Hay House Publishers India, Muskaan Complex,
Plot No.3, B-2, Vasant Kunj, New Delhi 110 070
Tel: (91) 11 4176 1620; Fax: (91) 11 4176 1630; www.hayhouse.co.in



A catalogue record for this book is available from the British Library.

Tradepaper ISBN: 978-1-4019-6067-4
E-book ISBN: 978-1-78817-399-5
Audiobook ISBN: 978-1-78817-606-4

Interior illustrations: 70 (top): Shutterstock/Okvov; 70 (bottom): Shutterstock/ AVA Bitter; 261: headshot of Natalia by Andie Redmond; headshot of Terry by Sophie Ziegler

10 9 8 7 6 5 4 3 2 1

Printed in the United States of America

*To our children, Sequoia, Ossian and Bede.*

# Contents

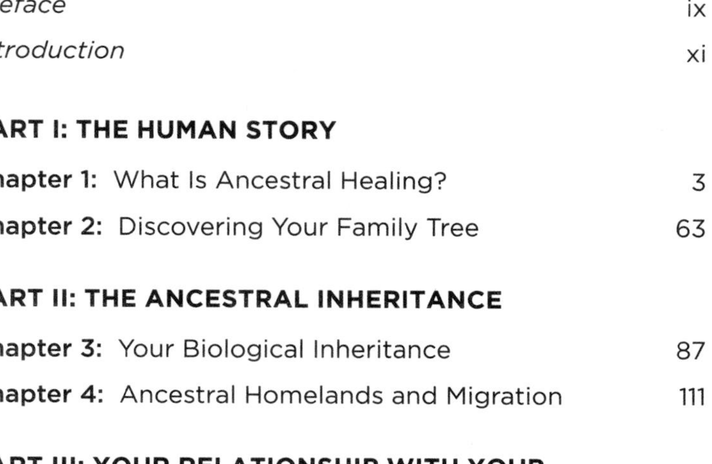

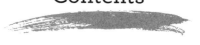

# Preface

This book is made accessible for all readers from those with little or no personal experience of ancestral healing to the more advanced practitioners. Within these pages, we offer an in-depth and down-to-earth guide to ancestral healing practices. The book includes a wide range of meditations, healing techniques and rituals to heal, honour and remember our ancestors.

We live in a society that constantly refers to 'experts', forgetting our own personal life experiences and relationships with family members do actually qualify us to be able to address the ancestral healing practices taught in this book ourselves. What we find is that people just need a little encouragement if they're to awaken the ancestral healer within and use their gifts with confidence.

# Introduction

This book is a journey through the labyrinth of personal ancestral heritage, guiding everyone, regardless of whether they have spiritual beliefs or not, to draw on the power of the ancestors. Whether you put your trust in God and an afterlife, or in science and genetics, the power of those who went before you can be a guiding force in the life ahead of you.

By discovering our family history in addition to our DNA, ethnicity and culture, we can recognize the wonderful and the terrible truths about our roots. This knowledge can help us to understand more about who we are and this book offers powerful tools to heal the effects of genetic memories on our wellbeing. Through this awareness, we can begin to appreciate our personal restrictions, behaviours and intrinsic beliefs about the world around us. Most importantly, we can learn why and how negative influences and traumas passed down through our family lineage can affect not only relationships and our physical and mental health, but also our spiritual connections.

Even gifts and talents are inherited attributes that often skip generations. Even if our living relatives don't display any interest in our chosen direction, or might even seem positively opposed to it, we might well discover a personality further back who has the same talents and gifts as we do. Some of us are lucky enough to be born to a family where our innate talents and unique personalities are naturally encouraged and nurtured by those around us, while others aren't.

It's never too late to retrieve our own creative path and to heal the wounds and conditions that run through our family tree. By being aware that we're reflecting the same issues our family learned and inherited, we can then identify these influences, which can have tremendous value in gaining a deeper understanding of ourselves. In learning about family heritage, we can start to understand how we're affected by our family and find ways to heal their influences.

There are practices, rituals, exercises and meditations that can be applied to work with your inheritance, which can help you to embrace what's positive and heal what's negative. From here, you'll have the capacity to decide whether to continue with those patterns and in effect pass them on to the next generation, or you can resolve to make a break from the past. Furthermore, you'll gain an understanding of your relationship with the ancestors by connecting with them, communicating with them and honouring them.

If you suffer from any mental health issues and/or are grieving for a loved one, then this may not be the time for you to work on the darker aspects of your family heritage. If this is the case, it's an area of ancestral healing you can return to when you're able to address those traumas that you and your family may have experienced in the past.

## Our story

Our interest in the spirit world and ancestors started when we were young. We always had a feeling there's an existence beyond this Earth.

### *Terry O'Sullivan*

Just after the Second World War, we were living with my grandparents. I shared a bedroom with my parents and I remember having to remain silent because my grandfather in the adjoining bedroom had to get up at 5 a.m. for work. As a young boy, I remember seeing both 'people' and 'things' that others couldn't. Nobody understood or cared about what I 'saw' and they'd call it my 'make-believe' world.

After we moved away, the images began to fade, coinciding with when I was gearing up to find my place in the world. I had, in fact, almost forgotten my earlier experiences with make-believe and it was only when I had one during Holy Communion at the local Catholic Church (my father was Catholic) that my interest was again kick-started by the theological mysteries, such as encounters with angels and the unseen world of spiritualism.

If I told anybody I'd seen an angel, nobody would have believed me. But I had, and I'd also experienced the sensation of being lifted out of my body into a dominion of great light. My secret world continued to be illuminated by visions and dreams. The only person I could turn to was Grandma Cooke, my maternal grandmother. She was a teller of fortunes whose mother was a pureblood Romany gypsy, and at last I found I was able to share my make-believe world, through which I discovered an ancestral legacy that would instinctively guide me. The years that followed enabled me to accept fully my make-believe world as a reality.

I began with spiritualism, and it was this teaching that helped me to hone my skills to see the dead more clearly and learn how to rescue earthbound spirits. This was followed by an opportunity to embrace Native American traditions, in which I learned how we're strongly connected to the land. In these teachings, I observed that the Earth is our ancestral legacy – that we are born, live, die and return to our origins. This gave me the breadth and depth of knowledge and experience that I later introduced to my practices as a soul rescuer.

Following these teachings, I discovered Tibetan Buddhism. It was then I learned how important it is to recognize humanity and the impermanence of all things. Native American beliefs taught me that the place of death and the walk of life are inseparable. It was the wisdom of Tibetan Buddhism that aroused in me a trust that I could believe in both life and death, and the idea that I'll continue to have a purpose even after death.

In Africa, it was only when I was alone in the Kalahari Desert that I realized I'd been on a journey of an awakening of my spiritual gifts. I was then initiated in the ancient traditions of tribal Africa as a sangoma – a shaman and healer. The principles of their tradition are based on ancestral communications and the ancestors were consulted to give me a name that suited my gifts, my life. The name I was granted was Dabulamanzi, meaning 'an opener of doors', which made me realize we must keep the door open to the ancestors so they may reach out and touch us. In return, we may recognize that we're all strongly connected, like a string of prayer beads.

### *Natalia O'Sullivan*

Throughout my career as a healer and spiritual therapist, I discovered that we all suffer from ancestral dysfunctions or wounds that deserve to be healed. By addressing our ancestral past, we learn to transform the legacy of our ancestors.

During my work as a mediator for the deceased, I've been profoundly moved by the transformations I've witnessed. The reconciliation, healings and reconnection achieved between my clients and their ancestors have revealed the establishment of an ongoing legacy that can be handed down to both current and future generations.

When it comes to my own story, my parents changed our family's legacy by moving to Britain. My mother grew up in Spain during the Spanish Civil War, which was a time of great tragedy for many. My grandfather was among those directly affected, when in 1938 he was executed for being against the Franco regime. My grandmother was left bereft and grieving for most of her life.

During the 1960s and 70s, countless families left Spain for economic rather than political reasons, many of whom came to Britain. My mother followed her sister, Teresa, and came to the UK during the early 1960s, where she met my father. My father was born in Hungary in the 1930s and grew up during World War Two. After the war, Hungary itself suffered a great deal as a result of having allied with Germany. Notably, Hungary became occupied by Communist Russia. This meant families like my own who were landowners and farmers were persecuted and had their lands confiscated. My father fled his home country age 18 during the 1956 Hungarian Uprising and travelled across Europe as a refugee to Britain. This short but decisive period in history massively impacted my father's side of the family.

## Becoming an ancestral healer – Natalia's journey

Throughout my life, my relationship with my family has been an emotional one, but it's always been guided and supported by my spiritual relationship with my ancestors. Since childhood, they've come to me in dreams, through spoken and unspoken thoughts and premonitions, either before a child is conceived, or when family members require help or guidance. My gift came from being born to a family who were accomplished in the skills of ancestral communication and healing. I'm the chosen one from my generation to inherit this skill. Within a family of gifted psychics or healers, there's often a chosen child who inherits these gifts, but with this come burdens.

As a child, I knew I was supersensitive on every level. I could see, hear, sense and touch so much information that was going on that was unspoken and unseen by others. I was overwhelmed by everything around me. Not only could I sense and experience premonitions, but I could also hear and feel what people were thinking and gauge their mood without them saying anything. If someone held my hand or touched me, I could sense their energy and read their thoughts. Often, it could make me unhappy or unwell.

I could also feel the grief and loss my grandparents had experienced. It was particularly profound when we visited one another, when I could sense the pull of family stories, along with unspoken depths of despair and grief. When I stayed in their homes, the ancestors would come to me at night, leaving me feeling invaded by their thoughts, feelings and unresolved issues.

Besides reading people, I could also sense if someone was ill. Even if the illness hadn't yet manifested, I could tell if someone was going to die or if they were close to death.

This overwhelming sense of grief would come over me and I'd want to cry deep, long tears. I could feel them telling me they knew they weren't going to be here much longer. When we visited my friend's father, I knew without him saying anything, just a look he gave me that day, that this was the last time I'd see him. He died a few days later.

Certain houses and places made me fearful, as I could sense the family's dead relatives. I now know they were only trying to communicate with me. Ancestors generally move on, but some remain around their family for their own reasons and many come to help their living descendants. By the time I was a teenager, I decided this had to stop. I recognized that there must be a way to resolve the fears and anxieties – I knew they weren't mine and that I was being what they call 'overshadowed'.

I undertook my training in mediumship and spiritual healing in Richmond with Gilly Griffiths, a spiritual medium and healer. It was there that I eventually met my husband, Terry, when he was running workshops for her students on spirit rescue. The more I looked into my relationship with my own ancestors and supported the healing of those of others, the more my anxieties and fears began to wane.

I soon discovered my passion for ancestral healing, which would become my profession. Through my own story, I understand how to heal intergenerational trauma. As descendants of a family who suffered through war, genocide and famine, I recognize that we manifest both mental and physical problems through ancestral inheritance. My singular focus and enthusiasm in this field continues to grow ever stronger as I work with others to address their own stories and heal their own personal ancestral inheritance. In turn, this enables them and their loved ones - past, present, and future - to live fuller, healthier, happier lives.

### *Our meeting*

I (Natalia) met Gillian Griffiths when I was 19 years old. While studying with Gilly for a couple of years, I began to have a lot of really difficult psychic encounters, during which I frequently came to class with stories of haunted houses and numerous confrontations with ancestral relatives and ghosts. Gilly helped me to become adept at assisting the spirits to move on until I became involved in a particular haunting that was far too malevolent for our psychic and spiritual skills. It was then that she suggested introducing me to a friend of hers who was a renowned ghost hunter, soul rescuer and healer - Terry O'Sullivan. This was 1984.

The workshop Gilly organized saw the beginning of my relationship with Terry. We made our connection through a spiritual interest and I began my initiation in soul rescue work with him. Since then, we've travelled across the world and visited hundreds of homes, helping people to heal their ancestral heritage, releasing the souls of the dead and healing the Earth. We've worked with individuals and their families for many years with the main purpose of teaching and creating space for people to address their family's wounds and inherited issues. By encouraging their own personal healing, we help them begin to resolve the wounds of those who came before them, and thereby current family conflicts and problems, changing the legacy of their family's future so it may become more positive, supportive, healthy and liberated.

Together, we wrote books on soul rescue and ancestral healing to offer people the opportunity to understand the realms of spirit and that deep connection we all have with our ancestors. Since the physical and the spiritual co-exist, beliefs throughout the world confirm that physical death is but a rite of passage to the liberation of the spirit into the light and the ancestral realms.

# Part I

# THE HUMAN STORY

Chapter 1

# What Is Ancestral Healing?

*'When I work with people, I ask them to shake the family tree to see what falls out, what secrets have been hidden, what story has never been told, what trauma has never healed all the way.'*

MARK WOLYNN

Ancestral healing is an intention with purpose to release the shadows, wounds and unresolved traumas from our ancestral lineage, healing our family tree. The shadows of the powerful relationship we share with our ancestors can have a subtle impact on our psychological and emotional behaviours. A story will begin to emerge as you unravel and compare your own characteristics and ancestral conditions. As you uncover the roots of your ancestors in your family heritage, patterns will become obvious as you delve into seemingly irrational fears and psychological, emotional and physical difficulties.

Naturally, both your childhood and adult relationships are all affected by the way your family have raised you. This is even the case if you've been adopted or brought up by a single parent, whether or not you know who your family are. Biological and genetic relationships play an important part in how you feel about yourself. The aim of ancestral healing is to address the influences coming through from biological inheritance, which can potentially have an intrinsic effect on behaviours and beliefs. At the same time, these influences are extrinsically shaped by the environment in which we've been born and raised. However, it's the combination of conditioning and inheritance that affects how we perceive ourselves and how we conduct our relationships with others. This is the reality of our ancestral legacy.

As we cannot control who brings us into this world, we cannot sway how we're raised or force the culture we've been born into to become welcoming to us, but we can transform the way we think about all these things. We can choose to be determined and start the process of healing with an intention. It's we who create the actions needed to resolve any or all of these issues with our family.

## Why now?

Our society is now in the labour pains of a new age of environmental responsibility. We're having to deal with climate change, the fear and hopelessness of confronting the possibility of the annihilation of humankind, gender and race inequalities, national and international crises, and political and financial catastrophes, all of which are creating a turning point in our story as human beings.

These many crises stem from a societal lack of a sense of connection to a spiritual lineage. It's this connection that should be an anchor to help give us courage and faith in the face of great difficulties. Many have lost the appreciation that we're all part of a sacred continuum. Equally, we're also descendants of both our own ancestors and of those who follow.

Furthermore, the connection to our ancestral past has been taken over by the wake of immense changes that have occurred over the past 150 years. Mobility has changed the face of our social cultural values and how we relate to different generations in our family. What we call the sanctity of the home has been replaced by a mobile society. Families are now more isolated, which affects younger as well as older generations, in that we no longer have the support of extended family. Many children often don't know their extended family members and aren't aware of how it feels to be part of a larger clan.

This will of course influence who we are, as we're all part of this interconnectedness with society. Learning what's expected of us at this crucial time is therefore essential. Awareness of the line of connection between the generations - past, present and future - urgently needs to be re-established to prevent adverse social and cultural influences that will in turn impact gravely on our society in the future.

Teaching our children about a sense of tradition and gaining a knowledge of who they are as part of a family group and where their family came from will promote feelings of security in the face of difficulties. Most of us are neglectful and unaware of how much our ancestral family support both our lives and those of our descendants. If we could acknowledge their presence, it would greatly enhance our sense of peace and wellbeing.

In most traditions, it's taught that the ancestors have a rightful place within the lives of their descendants. Even their names are passed on to their descendants, as well as their wisdom, gifts and talents. Their occupations, religious practices and moral beliefs all serve as guidance on how they should conduct themselves within their family, extended family, community and wider society as a whole.

Our ancestors were able to assimilate transitions into their lives because new events, challenges and rites of passage from puberty to death were honoured. They were incorporated in the present patterns using tradition and ritual. Unlike today, when we're overwhelmed by many sources of ever-changing and often frightening news, our ancestors passed on the 'news' in the form of stories told around evening tribal fires; potential problems and current events were discussed and evaluated in light of their ancestral history. A sense of tradition and collective memories of past successes as well as failures would be surpassed by the awareness of the line of connection between all the generations. When observed, this tradition instils a sense of continuum that gives us a greater understanding of who we are and where we've come from.

## Why it matters

Both ancestral wisdom and wounding can be passed on and can last for generations. By entering the 'right relationships' with them, you can enlist the help of your ancestors to clear old wounds and unresolved issues. The ancestors cannot help you unless you let them and if you don't ask them for their help, none will come. In acknowledging their existence, a continuum between the living and the dead can provide a link with the past that both inspires and supports.

The whole point to ancestral healing is to understand that we're the carriers of old stories in new bodies, using contemporary ideas to deal with it all. The ancestors left their troubles behind to be picked up by us as their own unfinished business. It wasn't always their intention to leave the kind of legacies they did. Sometimes it was down to unavoidable circumstances, other times a series of poor decisions.

Even if our ancestors' lives were tragic, there's still something within their existence that's of value. Perhaps an untapped, unused, unlived gift or talent, or a strength or virtue they've passed on. It's useful to discover the stories about our ancestors, even if it only goes back to our grandparents. We can then systematically reveal to the world who these people were, to give them a kind of continued life. As such, we can examine the things that were important to them and aim to bring those very qualities into our own lives.

A family is kept alive by its history. If we can pass on the stories that matter as well as the tales that seem less fertile, the tapestry of truth and myth, usually in equal parts, enables descendants to explore the parallels between their own lives and those of their ancestors. There are too many families who unintentionally or otherwise keep their histories hidden. This might resonate as a dark secret that nobody talks about, or a medical condition that's been inherited and can be passed on again in the future. Importantly, such information may help to avoid guilt, shame and embarrassment when it comes to how others view your family history owing to their own, or even help to save lives when illnesses and health issues are revealed. If we can be truthful and not hide skeletons in our cupboard, if we can overcome the shame or scandal of our forebears, it would make life so much easier for our descendants to make peace, come to terms with and even forgive the mistakes and transgressions of earlier generations.

Imagine your heritage to be linked together like prayer beads, with each bead recording the exploits of each family member. The prayer beads are all linked together, connected to each other and made inseparable by their very connection. Each bead retains its own story but is passed to the next prayer bead, as in the seed of bloodline. These stories are just like the seeds of reproduction we inherited and would become the cause of an inheritance carried into the next generation. Some of us will be lucky, others not so fortunate in what they inherit.

After exploring your roots, the next step is the discovery of your ancestral patterns. Some of the negative legacies from our predecessors can have a staggering and overwhelming effect on our behaviours and emotions. If these aren't addressed, they can cause negative familial patterns that affect relationships between family members. To instigate change, we need to alter family patterns that dwell within each of us.

This means we must take time to develop positive influences and to work at healing negative familial patterns to change the attitudes, beliefs and identities of our own generation. In turn, this will help to create a new collective unconscious, which is essential for the continuity of life on our planet.

## Your ancestral healing journey

To embark on this journey, you must review your life from the beginning. This can feel daunting as you begin to see how you leave one phase for another: progressing from childhood to adolescence to young adulthood and beyond. During our lifetimes, we'll experience the turbulence of partnerships and perhaps marriage, with periods of being single. We'll move from middle age to old age, facing the prospect of death and loss. It's in these transitions that we'll leave relationships and the home of our parents behind, abandoning outmoded values, discovering our talents and professional direction along the way. We'll search for opportunities as we seek out those we wish to love and uncover our passions, all the way ascertaining who we really are.

This is like peeling away layers of an onion, the different stages of our lives bringing completely different influences and experiences. What kind of narrative has your life been? Do you see it as a drama? Or as an adventure? Do you experience one crisis after another? Or has it been rather insular or isolated?

## Ancestral notebook

Buy a notebook to record any dreams, insights and inspiration you have while exploring your ancestral lineage. These thoughts and ideas will be useful when going through later exercises in this book.

The ancestral notebook is designed to accompany you on your journey. Use it to record all the information that you find out about your family and its history. Writing everything down in one place will provide the raw material from which to draw your family tree. As you continue, you'll begin to see familial patterns emerging.

- Begin with yourself and the facts as you know them: date of birth, baptism, marriage, where you've lived and schools attended.
- Write a short biography, including any significant incidents involving members of your family.
- In addition, record any thoughts and feelings that come to mind about other people, such as school friends or neighbours. This will be an interesting record for you later in life, as well as for future generations, and it may help you to identify events and relationships you'd like to explore further.

- Repeat this process for your parents and grandparents. If you don't already have documents and information to work from, check the accuracy of the various dates with them and ask them about their lives, noting important dates, people and events.
- If you're planning to have a family of your own, investigate your partner's background. Include relationships with half-siblings and stepfamily, as this will also have an impact on the ancestral healing process.
- If you're adopted, both the biological and the adoptive or foster family will have an influence. Give some thought as to where your strongest connections lie and add them to this process.
- Ask family friends and extended family what they remember about deceased relatives. What were they like when they were alive? What were their best and worst traits?

Once you've recorded everything about your immediate family, you may want to start looking back at earlier generations.

---

Members of our family may tell us we take after someone in a previous generation. Perhaps we have the same hair colour, distinctive nose or unusually large hands. These are obvious examples of physical characteristics, but what we're looking for are other patterns, such as details from those who lived through historical and dramatic events, or interesting behaviours, talents and gifts. Our own life story will undoubtedly reflect that of our ancestral stories as we experience various life transitions from childhood to adulthood and so on. As we go through these different and sometimes difficult stages, unbeknown to us, certain members of our own ancestral family would have experienced similar traumas.

It's in the discovery of how they managed these trials that you'll determine how you feel about your own experiences. In turn, you'll discover how you'll respond to these challenges. You may decide certain things fill you with fear or anxiety, or you may find the determination to succeed and the courage to push on through life's adventures.

During this process of uncovering ancestral stories, we often discover why we don't like or connect with our family and instead search for other family groups or types of communities. This is especially evident in those who have grown up in a dysfunctional environment, because they'd have developed strategies to survive and overcome the trials in their upbringing.

Many find that if they can change their family's circumstances, such as through marriage or migration, they can summon the resilience to surround themselves with people who love and support them unequivocally. They may choose partners and family members they can feel safe with and supported by, letting go of those who continue to hurt and abuse them. At times, the love and the blood that glues everyone together can be stronger than personal issues. Habitually, many of us still return home to heal and forgive, to receive love and support. Sometimes it seems almost impossible to heal some of those dysfunctional family relationships. However, the courage of being able to look back at our family past will give us the skills to know how to move forwards with our current family relationships.

## Healing the family tree

The family tree is a timeframe in which the ancestral lineage can be mapped out from the last generation to earlier ones, connecting your family to an assembly of names. Discovering familial patterns makes us realize that they both enhance and obstruct our personal destiny. By reaching into our inheritance, we can study generational blueprints and make a break with the past. Ancestral stories transmitted to our subconscious can affect us deeply. For example, ancestors who have died suddenly or under traumatic circumstances send reverberations through the family tree, so each generation suffers the pain of loss. It's the same with all forms of generational legacy, from famine and poverty to war and genocide. But sometimes it's in the daily chores we engage in or the status and education of our family that claim our inheritance.

Whether you're overshadowed by ancestral memories or affected by collective family trauma, there are various ways to help heal the past. It begins by exploring our family history and recognizing what we ourselves have inherited, particularly from our parents and grandparents. When people come to see us for a consultation for the first time, they often meet the one ancestor they least expected. But the family member who caused the most pain and dysfunction is invariably the one who holds the key to healing the past. And the one who tried their best to support their children and descendants is often the one who was unable to stop the legacy from being passed on.

When Desi came to see Natalia, her mother had just died and it was a very emotional session. Desi came to the UK when she was 12 and they've lived here ever since. Her family was from Bulgaria and her mother was Turkish. Desi graduated in Film Studies and is now working as a documentary filmmaker and podcast host. Her sister is also very successful, gaining a PhD and working as a scientist at a London university. Desi wanted to understand why she and her sister felt like their achievements were never quite good enough and why there was a feeling of not deserving something more in life:

### Desi's story

*The very first time I communicated with my mother through Natalia after she died, I realized just how many things my mum was still holding on to during her life that she hadn't shared with us. I guess it was her way of protecting us or not wanting to bring up old memories that had been buried, but it was clear how much this emotional baggage was weighing her down, and no doubt contributed to her illness.*

*After my mother's death, I wanted to investigate my family's history and how that affected both her generation and mine. Looking at the past and the patterns of those who came before us makes you see things differently. My mum was always a workaholic. After we moved to the UK, to make ends meet she took two jobs so we could afford not only all the expenses, but also the mortgage for the house we'd always dreamed of. There was always a fear present in her of 'not having enough', which I guess came from her childhood experience of poverty. However, as I began to investigate her side of the family, I realized it was more than just a fear of being poor.*

*Coming from a typical Turkish background, their mentality was extremely focused on the idea of being 'good' and 'hardworking'. There were so many times that my grandmother told us stories of the good things people in her neighbourhood did, such as giving away food or sacrificing something of their own to help others. She'd tell us about the time she was pregnant with my mum and how she worked on the field up until she gave birth. There was so much pride that came with the idea of being a self-sacrificing person.*

*But in my mother's case, it was as if whatever she did still wasn't good enough, and she felt that she never quite measured up to other people's expectations. I could clearly see how this pattern was passed on from my grandmother to my mother, and now to my sister and me. Becoming conscious of these patterns and slowly putting an end to them was my first step towards healing the family tree.*

A positive action to change a negative ancestral pattern can begin with a small step. For instance, if there are workaholics on both sides of the family and you, too, are victim to this trait, a small action you could take is to make time to rest for an hour once a week. If you come from a family where everyone is extremely negative and critical, you may find yourself behaving in a similar way. Learning to stop responding with an automatic negative response will begin to make a difference to your thinking and lead you to incorporate changes in your daily lifestyle.

If you discover there have been some serious problems in your family such as addiction, abuse, secrets or shame, this will require more attention. You can address some of the health and psychological issues passed down the family line by way of family therapy or by having open and loving discussions with your family, even if they're resistant to discussing these hidden issues. Exploring them helps to heal the lineage rather than pretending the issues aren't there or hiding the truth.

Some of the most difficult patterns that are inherited are those of sexual roles that are passed down. Studies show that parents who abuse their children were themselves abused as children. People who have been abused have been known either to collude with their abuser or change things, creating a new history for their own family. Although this area of inheritance isn't one that most relatives want to discuss or acknowledge, it's valuable to pursue this investigation for yourself. Addressing the sexual behaviours and attitudes of one generation could dramatically influence those of the next.

## Creating new patterns

Every time you change or release a negative family pattern, you create a new identity. This new sense of self will in turn change the current dynamics of your relationships. The most difficult aspect of healing ancestral patterns is being able to allow you and your family to form this new identity, which means being able to view life differently, becoming more positive and less afraid. Baby steps in lifestyle changes and undertaking therapy are great ways of healing your ancestral patterns. Our identities are so interwoven with those of our family that we need time away from them to get to know who we are without them.

Often, if your family are happy with the way they are, as you heal and change you can feel like a stranger. This is to be expected and it'll pass as you start to find your new identity and begin setting boundaries when it comes to how you want to be within your family unit. Other families, however, are supportive and welcoming of change.

When we're born to a family, we enter a complex matrix of relationships. Our ancestral history can cloud our personal awareness of our true self and shadows from childhood can dictate the way we think, just as our parents were clouded by the views of their parents and so on. Sometimes we absorb an ancestor's story into our own and it's difficult to know how to separate ourselves from the issues that plague our family. The journey is one of evolution and each step, each ritual, each healing, each prayer takes us closer to the lives our ancestors are dreaming for us.

## Identifying with your childhood memories

As we grow up, what we must rely on is correct advice and guidance. If we aren't given good advice about who we are when we're children, then later, things won't make sense. This leads many of us to question the credibility of what we've been told or we end up doubting ourselves.

### Evelyne's story

*Evelyne Valabregue is a French biodynamic psychotherapist who works with family and ancestral wounds and she has the following to say:*

*I've worked on family inheritance with my clients. Their present woundedness is always a repetition of what they felt as a child when it came to one of the parents' behaviours. What's happened is that it's been internalized and sometimes has been for generations. All relationship problems stem from relations to the parents. When the client becomes aware of the wound, criticism and inappropriate behaviours, they realize they're replaying this role with their partner. As such, they can then take back their power and find new ways of being, and the relationship changes. Becoming aware of this process enables them to have other responses. The old hurts, fears, negativity and abuse are still there in their psyche for a while, but they stop becoming a part of the client's identity. They're now able to allow themselves what they need and to fill their own hearts, thereby stopping the unconscious family legacy.*

The memories we pass on are those we carry in ourselves and if they're not released or laid to rest, they can fester as a niggle, an emotional grievance or a physical blemish that goes unrecognized and misdiagnosed, endangering both our lives and those of our descendants. The physical body is complicated enough without all these hidden agendas. The brain is a store cupboard, a memory bank with all its secrets, which can drive us crazy if we keep them to ourselves.

## Once you see it, we can heal it

*'Those so-called "black sheep", the ones that don't fit, the ones that howl with rebellion, actually repair, detox and create new thriving branches in their family tree.'*

BERT HELLINGER

If we could change some of our limiting core beliefs, this would create an energy that emanates from within us, touching the hearts and souls of those around us, like ripples in a still pool. As we begin to feel as if we're on a continuum with those left behind us, this could help to transform their behaviours as well as affect our present relationships and those of our future descendants. Mira is from Serbia and here's how she changed her family legacy:

### Mira's story

*I know now that I'm a descendant of ancestors who knew violence, poverty, betrayals, hardships, disillusionments, disappointments and suffering very well. In our own way, my sister and I have worked to change family tendencies over the last 20 years. She succeeded very well financially, while I made leaps of progress both emotionally and spiritually. At our dad's deathbed, I swore I wouldn't live a suppressed and hard life like him, and I hope he's proud of what I've achieved so far. I also don't think I'd have been able to make progress had I stayed in Serbia. Dark, oppressive, violent forces of the land would have locked me in and disabled me in my healing journey.*

When you've suffered trauma, you often shut away that memory, as it's too much for you to cope with at that time. You learn to protect your vulnerability by forgetting. However, these frozen memories remain inside you. Sometimes you need to go back to places where you've lived or that hold memories for you, both good and bad. Going back helps you to face what's happened and heal the soul loss that was caused by what you experienced. These could all still be held as traumatic memories inside you that can only be repaired by applying the 'once you see it, you can heal it' principle. Seeing the past as the person you are today, not the person you once were, essentially leads to retrieving your soul loss.

For example, Victoria loved but resented her adoptive father. He was a closed book and would never discuss anything emotional. He was unaffectionate and while he encouraged her academic studies, his way of showing his love for her was by telling family and friends how proud he was of her. She also had a difficult and emotionally abusive relationship with her adoptive mother, which didn't help how she felt about her childhood. She felt isolated and unloved.

For her to be able to change the way she felt about herself, she had to let go of the critical and unhappy childhood memories. She began to look at how and when her adoptive parents did love and support her. Realizations such as how they'd encouraged her academic and professional career and how she was now a successful theatre director were helpful. Furthermore, Victoria acknowledged that her mother, who was brought up by critical Presbyterian parents, was actually unable to show affection and encouragement towards her. Because of her own upbringing, if her mother experienced something pleasurable, she was unable to recognize it.

Psychological research has shown that thinking positively can help to rewire the brain. Instead of feeling overwhelmed by the challenges one faces, one can find meaning within them and resolutions to them. Every transition teaches us something important if we allow it to. When your upbringing has been challenging and traumatic but loving, there are memories you can return to, so you can start to replace the negative ones with more positive ones.

A 2011 psychological study into gratitude and wellbeing conducted by Matsuba and Prikachin[1] divided 293 adults seeking mental health counselling into three groups. The first were asked to write letters of gratitude for three weeks. The second were asked to write about their deepest thoughts and feelings on negative experiences, and the final group didn't write anything. Those who wrote letters of gratitude reported significantly better mental health 12 weeks after the exercise. There was no change in mood in the other groups. Researchers have suggested that the practice of gratitude helped the group to let go of toxic emotions by reframing negativity in a productive way. They concluded that revisiting a memory of gratitude could make someone more sensitive to the experience in the future, which contributed to longer-lasting improved mental health and reframed the way they viewed their lives.

Shadows can be healed. We have the power to change the way we feel about ourselves and what's affected us from childhood by thinking about our relationships with our parents or primary caregivers. We can do this by looking back at the ages where there were significant memories of both good and bad times.

Bring to mind your own past and create a gratitude letter to the ancestors in the next exercise, starting with your parents and grandparents. If you're adopted or fostered, refer to your primary caregivers, not your biological family, as this addresses the experiences you had while growing up with your family, not just your inheritance.

## Identifying childhood memories

- On a large piece of paper, write down a timeline from birth to today's date.
- List on one side of the timeline positive memories and on the other your traumatic experiences.
- Record your age and dates alongside each of the aforementioned, so you begin to form a sort of chart.
- Once you've completed the chart, select photographs and memorabilia that remind you of these times.
- Lay everything out to stir up your memories.
- Next, light a candle or some incense or choose some aromatherapy oils to suit your mood.
- Sit in a comfortable position with your back straight. Breathe in through the nose and out through the mouth for a few minutes to relax.

- Keep your eyes closed and focus your mind on your breathing.
- With intention for your healing, out loud or in your mind, ask your ancestral guardian, God or spirit to help you investigate and heal your past.
- Visualize yourself returning to different times in your life on your timeline.
- Write in your journal how you remember each experience now, including everything you thought or felt.
- You may feel you need to address some of these wounds by returning to the more traumatic events with a therapist or healthcare professional.
- Return to this meditation regularly to work through different times and various emotions.
- The more you remember from the past, the more you will uncover that requires healing, thus the deeper the healing.
- Additionally, write a letter to all those who have loved and supported you.
- Thank them and state the reasons why.
- Write another letter to all those who have hurt and angered you, releasing your emotional attachment to them.
- Forgiveness and letting go are powerful ways of setting us free from the past and healing past traumas.
- Place both of these letters on your altar (*see page 30*) and give thanks.

---

Disconnecting from those who caused your pain is about setting yourself free. This process can transform your relationship with both living and deceased relatives who were involved with some of these difficult or traumatic memories. When we cannot forgive them, we can forgive ourselves instead for allowing ourselves to be hurt and for holding on to these past situations. Releasing the emotional charge to these events or connections to the person is fundamental to retrieving a healthy soul memory. Peace comes from letting go and forgiveness is key to healing ancestral pain.

## Ancestral healing practices

Within the ancient traditions of ancestral healing are several gifts we inherit as the mediators and healers for our family. One is being able to communicate with the ancestors to draw their spiritual support and protection for our family. Another is being able to confront death and transform fear into hope. Furthermore, it's being able to rescue those within our family tree who have abandoned the light and become earthbound.

We don't need to be able to communicate with the dead to help heal our ancestral inheritance. Everyone can make a difference, from planting a tree to creating a legacy. The important part is the return to the ancient tradition of respect when it comes to the best of what's been handed down to us, combined with a concern for what will come after us.

We can heal much of our family dynamic that comes from family history through simple rituals and by uniting the family at these times. Lucia is from Slovakia and now lives in London with her family. After experiencing a mild form of post-natal depression and anxiety, she brought the family together. Thoughts and feelings she'd had during her childhood resurfaced after giving birth to her son. When her sister, who already had two children, revealed that she, too, had experienced similar anxieties, fears and worries after the birth of her children, Lucia realized she wanted to do something about what was affecting her maternal lineage. She began with her mother, by addressing what had happened to her family:

### Lucia's story

*When I was growing up, I observed a lot of blame, a lack of accountability, the absence of forgiveness and a sense of injustice. There was a general hatred directed towards men and a tendency to blame them for everything. I became aware that there were four generations of women with dysfunctional partnerships, in turn becoming more controlling. There seemed a broad failure to connect with the strength of the maternal lineage, which was further limited by reliving the past ancestral heritage.*

*Motherhood led me to address my maternal lineage, as I realized I had to learn to balance tendencies towards feeling a loss of control and my distrust issues when it came to those I cared about most with healing the wounded aspects of my maternal line. As a result, one weekend when both my mum and my sister were visiting, I invited them to join me in a simple ancestral ritual. We sat round a fire and started the ritual with a meditation, during which we visualized all of our ancestors from the maternal side coming to us and hugging us. We thanked them for their gifts and one by one, we experienced their power, warmth and love, both from those we knew and those before them who we didn't.*

*After the meditation, I asked them to write down and share what we'd experienced, including those aspects that we wished to release both collectively and individually. We then burned the sheets of paper in the fire, in the knowledge that we now understood we have the power within to heal so our children and their children in turn can be free of this legacy.*

*I sense there is less fear and anxiety now on my mother's side of the family. I believe I'm guided and being looked after. I also trust I now have the power of all generations within me. What I found was that the male side of the family weren't usually present in the family unit, either through death, addictions or simply by being an absent emotional presence. The family story began with my great-grandmother, who lost her husband when she was 24. He was killed by a drunken neighbour who attacked my great-grandfather with an axe as he was returning home from work.*

*My great-grandmother already had a difficult life. When she was four years old, she lost both of her parents; her mother while giving birth to her brother, when both she and the baby had died, and her father who never returned from the war. For my great-grandmother, her new family were everything to her, so after her husband was killed, she was left alone to look after their young daughter, as well as running a farm. My great-grandmother had many gifts and was incredibly beautiful, but when she grew older, she never left the house or did anything with her life, which was one of the many stories of regret and blame that run through my female line.*

*My grandmother was forced to marry a man who had a good job and income. Unfortunately, it turned out this wasn't the best marriage and she blamed a lot of her unhappiness on my great-grandmother. My mother was subsequently born to a family where the parents had no emotional connection and my grandfather escaped by working and drinking, while my grandmother took care of everything alone. My mother was very young when she married my father. Sadly, they also had little emotional connection, which led to my father using drink as an escape, and eventually to his death from alcoholism.*

*When I was pregnant with my son, I decided it was time to do something about healing this ancestral lineage.*

The most effective way to address unwanted inherited aspects of our family heritage is by conducting healing rituals and personal ceremonies. It's through these practices that we can heal family issues and support deceased loved ones who may need help to move further into the light. Living family members can also be encouraged to learn how to prepare their own rituals and ceremonies to honour the birth and death of family members.

## *Ancestral altars*

To create a space in which to conduct healing rituals, you first need to build an altar or shrine (*see page 30*), then you can add healing tools such as crystals, pendulums, incense and candles. These can be placed on your altar for when you want to conduct a healing meditation or ceremony, or for ancestral honouring practices. An altar is a central focus or sacred space for worship, prayer, ritual or offerings, whereas a shrine is where we honour a particular person, spirit, deity or other entity.

To prepare yourself to conduct ancestral healing rituals or meditations, normal practice is first to cleanse yourself and your space by engaging in a fast or by going on a cleansing diet. General housekeeping of the space to be cleared is also required. For further guidance, refer to Chapter 5 (*see pages 144–46*).

You can honour the space with flowers, a plant, stones, feathers or crystals that represent the Earth. Items such as pictures or symbols that embody your own cultural heritage can also be added.

### *Family altars*

Constructed inside your home, the altar is a focal point for your connection with the spirit world and ancestral realms. The altar can be set up on a small table in the main living room or in your bedroom or study – anywhere that will remind you that your ancestors are part of your daily life. It can be covered with a tablecloth or silk cloth, on which you can place all of your favourite family photographs and those of your ancestors. Leave a space for the other items you've gathered, and add photographs and items that represent your family and ancestral heritage. Terry and I have a wall on which we've hung family photographs and those of ancestors that we've either been given or found through our research.

To build and sustain a connection, conduct a daily practice at your family altar by lighting incense and saying a prayer over the photographs, asking for daily support to bring peace, love and healing for both yourself and your family. Cleanse the space regularly using incense and by burning sage (*see page 145*) to lift the atmosphere both in and around the altar.

The importance of an ancestral altar is that it symbolizes the doorway to our relationship with the ancestors. Set aside 10 minutes or more on a daily basis to connect consciously with them. A daily practice helps to bring focus and, by its repetition, serves to remind you of both your intentions and your relationship with your ancestral family.

For this next exercise, think about what you're looking to heal. Actively decide what guidance it is that you're seeking either for yourself or your family. Are there any family members who need help or healing? Has someone just died who needs support? Or does a newborn need assistance? If you have any objects that belong to your ancestors, hold each article one at a time and imagine yourself connecting with them. I use a necklace of my grandmother's and hold it while saying a prayer to her to ask for healing or support for my children. I can sense her presence around me and feel her patient strength filling me when I need her help.

## Meditation by the altar

- Make yourself comfortable and relax beside your altar.
- Empty your mind of your daily duties and let your thoughts wander, just as if you're daydreaming.
- Connect with quiet sounds, echoes and influences in your subconscious, such as memories and connections with your ancient past.
- Be open. Breathe and relax, and see what comes back to you.
- Write down in your journal what you sense, think or feel.
- Repeat this connection daily or at least once a week.

- Read about your ancestral heritage – its history, mythology, cultural music – and awaken that connection.
- Inspire your creativity to ignite your personal connection with your ancestral heritage.

---

### *The ancestral shrine*

When we build a shrine to the ancestors, we connect with shamanic traditions and the practices of our more ancient ancestors. They're known as the wisest and most powerful, superseding all blood and recent ancestral connections. The shrine serves as a focal point for both the community and the extended family.

In African traditions, on the eve of an important undertaking, the guardian priest requests that the shrine's doors open. Offerings are then made, which might include giving a sacrifice of thanks in the form of wine or food. The community don't just go to the shrine to ask for help – they go to give thanks. If there's been a ceremony, then the next day at dawn, the community will congregate to honour the ancestors.[2]

Traditional ancestral practices are performed around a circle that remains unbroken, as it contains the knowledge that without honouring the ancestors, there would be no life at all to celebrate. There are so many diverse stories around our origin when it comes to describing our ancestors' early existence. The roots of our ancestral lineage pinpoint a story of humanity that began long before records existed.

### *Building your shrine*

An ancestral shrine is more suited to being built in nature, as the purpose of one is to harness the Earth's energy. If you have a garden or a favourite place, you can simply construct a shrine with local stones, feathers, shells, or fallen branches or logs. Shape the shrine as a circle, with a flat surface on the top on which you can place symbols and pictures.

Use stones and crystals beneath the four corners so the shrine sits just off the ground. When choosing stones, take into account their different meanings depending on the purpose for creating the shrine - red stones reflect passion, blue stones indicate calm and creativity, and so on. Add plants and flowers that resonate with your family's cultural roots. You can even place archetypes from your ethnic culture, such as mythological gods, goddesses and deities, as well as things that represent nature spirits to you - such as mountains, trees, rivers, seas and rocks - and animal spirits.

Some people like to have a wood burner nearby on which to burn incense and for fire ceremonies. Pay homage to the ancestors by lighting candles, or adding gifts of flowers or plants. Ask for inspiration and guidance.

### *Creating a sacred space*

Creating a sacred space need not be limited to the home or garden or even the office - it can be accomplished in the most temporary of surroundings. Throughout history, sacred spaces have continued to be created in permanent settings with formal arrangements of large ritual objects and furniture, such as altars and benches, as well as impermanent ones with portable versions of sacred objects. A mobile altar can be created simply with a printed image or small statue, or a few stones, crystals and fossils. Choose whatever represents your own feelings and those of your family, including any of your own favourites, such a small piece of cloth and photographs or items from your ancestral family. This will enable you to feel at home both spiritually and emotionally in order to connect with your ancestral family.

Shrines are generally made in nature and can be either permanent fixtures made in stone or built from the ground using items such as stones, wood and clay. They're found all over the world, scattered amid the landscape, representing local gods, deities and ancestral spirits that live in that particular community. Altars and shrines can be erected where you currently live and the more portable they are, the better, especially if you and your family no longer live where your ancestors once did.

Whether we're shadowed by ancestral memories or affected by collective family trauma, there are various ways to help heal the past. It begins by exploring our family history and recognizing what we've inherited, particularly from parents and grandparents. With addressing the family's shadow comes an understanding of sensitivity and how to heal childhood wounds. Our inner child is the part of us that carries the emotional traumas from childhood and is influenced by the manner in which our parents or primary caregivers brought us up. They, too, have inherited ancestral shadows, having been affected by their own upbringing and the historical climate of their own childhood. This is reflected in their intrinsic prejudices and attitudes, often arising from their family's status, as well as cultural and religious beliefs.

### *Rituals and ceremonies*

Rituals and ceremonies used for ancestral healing are one of the most powerful catalysts for awakening inner power. They can be both creative and grounding, helping us to focus on what's affecting us in life. We can then use them to seek answers or find solutions to help us make changes. All rituals involve three stages: preparation, performance of rite and celebration.

Rituals used for ancestral healing can be designed to honour different levels of development and subsequent spiritual, psychological, emotional and physical changes that each transition in our life brings. The performance of a ritual is when we sit in meditation or prayer and summon a connection with our ancestors. Many light candles, burn incense, or write requests and questions to the ancestors and so on. These are then placed on an ancestral altar. Some people build fires and organize a ceremony with individual members of the family, and others go to their favourite places in nature to conduct meditations and rituals to honour ancestors.

You can create your own daily rituals and prayers in the form of a ceremony to provide the framework of how to make connections to your feelings and your own personal spirituality. This can be done either on your own or with family and friends to support and nourish each person's unique spiritual path and ancestral healing.

A ceremony or ritual doesn't have to come from any tradition but can bring new ideas to some traditional sacred practices such as prayers, dedications and healing rites, and even at births, marriages and funerals. The ancestors can help us to release the past and let go of what's wounded, controlled or dampened us. In other words, whatever it is that's made us feel weak, inadequate or fearful. And they can help us to focus on what we know needs changing and healing in our lives, enabling us to make a clear intention of finding new ways to move forwards. The ancestors can create opportunities for new beginnings and close or end things. It can be helpful to receive guidance from our ancestral family to inspire these fresh ideas and transformations in our lives.

## Simple practice on how to conduct a ceremony

When conducting a ceremony, you take on the role of the ancestral healer or family mediator. A ceremony is normally led by a priest or priestess and in this case, you as the family mediator.

Think about the reasons why you'd want to conduct a ceremony and the purpose behind it. As the ancestral mediator, you need to make all the arrangements, including sending out invitations. Give thought to how you'd like to celebrate or inspire your family to enjoy and empower the ceremony as you follow these next steps:

- Take time to be clear about your intention for holding the ceremony. For example, you might wish to help heal, manage and support living or deceased family members.
- Prepare by thinking about what it is you want to do and why. For example, you may feel drawn to assist with a birth, death or marriage. Or you might want to heal medical or mental health problems. Or perhaps you want to put right trauma of some kind caused by life's problems such as abuse. Or you may decide to assuage financial, social or community issues. Include other people in the process, not just yourself.
- Decide who you'd like to attend, then set a date and time to conduct the ceremony.
- Create a sacred space in which to bring everyone together and to acknowledge the ancestral family (*see page 34*).
- Start by deciding where you'd like to conduct the ceremony: by your shrine or altar, in an outdoor space in nature, at the family home, in a social environment.

- Decide what ritual practice and prayers you'd like to conduct. If they're personal to your family, or cultural, give thought to how best you can lend support to the ceremony.
- Begin by opening the ceremony with an invitation to family members both living and deceased to join.
- Ask that they come in loving kindness and with compassion for everyone in attendance.
- Perform a grounding exercise by breathing deeply in through the nose and out through the mouth, connecting mind and body.
- Give everyone the opportunity to say a prayer out loud or quietly in their mind – just a few words to honour the space and the reasons behind the ceremony.
- You might want to chant, sing, meditate, play music, beat a drum, ring a bell – anything that resonates. Perhaps engage in a guided visualization, or share a common focus of healing or prayer.
- You might even light a fire either inside or outside.
- Invite the positive spiritual energy that surrounds your family to join in.
- Offer gifts of flowers, wood and crystals to the ancestors. If you're inside, have a celebratory drink and offer food.
- When everyone has said a few words, give thanks, acknowledging everyone in attendance.
- Close the ceremony with a gratitude prayer to your ancestors. Breathe deeply in a relaxed manner, and in your own time open your eyes.
- Leave a gift for the spirit of place if you're outside, or place a gift on the fire or altar for your ancestral family.

---

## Healing the family shadow

To acknowledge that living family members sometimes aren't the only cause of these ancestral shadows is to accept there's an inheritance that links to disturbances in our family tree. Some more than others absorb an ancestor's life story into their own to the degree that they cannot see where the ancestor's story ends and their own begins because it's been with them for so long. For instance, some people suffer from all kinds of issues such as intimacy and commitment phobias, then find out their maiden aunt who died bitter and alone was abandoned by her lover. Or families who have difficulties with finances, who find it impossible to earn and save, may later discover a great-grandfather was an inveterate gambler who pitched the family into poverty.

Family shadows can be expressed in anxious words, fears, behaviours and unexplained physical symptoms. It's now understood this is inherited family trauma or secondary post-traumatic stress disorder (PTSD), leading to susceptibilities towards mental health problems. Even after the death of the person who suffered the original trauma, or whose stories have been forgotten or silenced, these memories and feelings live on.

These elements are carried as hidden memories, just like parts that make up the whole of who you are. But the shadows hide in secret places, in bones, blood and skin, all linked together in a subconscious landscape called the Dreamtime by the Aboriginal peoples of Australia. These factors are both learned by nurture and inherited by nature inside the body as if 'under the skin', making us feel uncomfortable, agitated or unhappy.[3]

Those who are suffering from intergenerational trauma tend to find it difficult to separate from family demands made by living family members. They don't want to adapt to family rules and traditions and may find themselves constantly trying to fit in but being judged or even rejected. These behaviours can cause all sorts of symptoms, which can make them feel they're unable to live their own lives without the shadow of their family's history.

According to the traditions of the indigenous people of Siberia and Mongolia, it takes approximately four generations or up to 100 years for the mental energy complex of an ancestor to disengage from this world completely. When this happens, the soul acquires the pattern of the most recent life just led. Everything a person has ever thought, felt, done or endured is recorded inside their DNA and this record is passed on. Therefore, when a child is conceived, they inherit the pattern derived from both their parents and their ancestors.

With the current revival of ancestral healing and from our own practice as healers, we're now beginning to recognize the spiritual and psychological value of much that our ancestors knew. We're learning to respect this ancient knowledge and understand its importance on our own health and wellbeing. In our experience in this field, we recognize that we can learn to understand how to translate these ancient healing practices into modern psychological and holistic approaches to healing our family inheritance.

In most ancestral healing practices, it's found that this memory can carry strong mental and emotional states from the ancestors, just as it can distort the emotional energy body of the newly forming individual. A new soul or baby who has just been conceived is the innocent and as such can only challenge this legacy. As a blank canvas, that innocence can be intruded on and certain personalities can challenge it. Some just give in without resisting the imposition of family shadows and conditioning. But if this new soul was strong enough to oppose it or, equally, become completely absorbed by it, they could in effect be empathetic enough to carry this inheritance. The key point when dealing with ancestral healing is that this family inheritance gives life to you. Whatever condition the energy is in, it'll determine the atmosphere in which you'll come into this world.

In some cases, children will show symptoms of inherited diseases early on in their lives. The immune system's ability to protect may diminish, meaning the physical body starts to show signs of inherited diseases the ancestors also suffered from. Conditions such as asthma, eczema and hay fever are the most common, but there are many other physical, mental, emotional and spiritual illnesses passed down from the ancestors that may begin to have an adverse effect on the physical body. For instance, as we become older, we become more like our parents and grandparents, and we start to recognize similarities of behaviours. We may find we begin to suffer from similar illnesses, as well as being affected mentally and emotionally from their sorrows, desires, fears, anxieties and lack of fulfilment from unaccomplished dreams.

It's important to understand that ancestral inheritance isn't about making you sick deliberately. Being unwell simply cannot be avoided, as it's an integral part of being a human being and belonging to a part of your family. Your predecessors may well have died from illnesses that afflicted them, but the root cause of disease is a breakdown in the body's energy system, which suggests that once something has gone awry with an ancestor's energy system, the condition remains even after the death of the physical body and can be passed through the family line.

The answer to our healing process lies in realizing that old ideas must constantly be removed. These may have been relevant to our parents, to our ancestors, but the key is in knowing when they're no longer relevant to us.

Perhaps it's only in subsequent generations that trauma can be witnessed and worked through, by those who weren't there to live it but who received its effects, belatedly, through the narratives, actions and symptoms of previous generations. For example, as is the case with my own family (Natalia), they might have suffered from experiences in their own historical and cultural stories. It doesn't matter that they've passed away – we can still inherit whatever conditions they had. As their descendants, through ancestral healing, we're offered the chance to heal whatever it is we've inherited from them. It takes courage, faith and self-awareness to change the dynamic of the intrinsic beliefs and conditions of our ancestors.

The good news is that there is a way of coming through the challenges of family dynamics, particularly when we realize we don't need to repeat the same patterns. Family, either living or dead, have a powerful effect not only on our self-esteem, but also on how we address our relationships both in childhood and later as adults. For every deliberation, we must consider the impact of our decisions on those around us. Our children learn how to conduct themselves in their relationships with others based on our interactions. The realm of influence reaches far beyond the boundaries of our immediate life, to the many with whom we've interacted throughout life. You may never know the impact you might have, but we can all change the world a little through our actions and experiences.

## Terry's story – my mother

I struggled to come to terms with my mother's behaviour. When I was growing up, she was not only emotionally abusive, but also fearful and anxious. This had a profound effect on me, as I was an only child with no other siblings with whom to share the impact my mother's behaviours had on the family. My father was always at work, so most of the time I was at home alone with her. It took a long time to be able to forgive her. It was only when I decided to look into her life and how she affected me so much during my childhood that I realized the root cause of my own issues.

It was at this point I recognized how she'd felt cheated by circumstances in her own life. She was only 15 when the war in Europe started and a mere 21 when the hostilities ceased. She was the youngest of four siblings with an exceedingly difficult older brother. Freddie, the youngest son, was her favourite brother. He died in the Second World War and his death affected her badly as they'd always been close and he was her confidant.

It was in observing the detail that I understood how his death would have left her feeling lonely and angry, diluted only with hate. She directed this only at those who had changed her life forever, such as the Japanese who had killed her brother. Consequently, she later created many difficult relationships, finding enemies in various situations.

In her lifetime, she never learned to forgive, which sadly made her hard-hearted. She expressed her fear in a belief that life would take everything from her that she valued and held dear. Her grief remained unresolved and she blocked her feelings, burying them deep inside and refusing to look at them again. Because of this she became afraid and unable to reconcile any feelings of loss, which she never came to terms with.

We encourage families to address their family's wounds and inherited issues. Through their personal healing, they can begin to remedy the wounds of those who came before them, changing the legacy of their family by inclusive forgiveness. Start by asking yourself the following questions:

- How do you really feel about your family?
- Are you close?
- How often do you communicate with each other?
- How often do you see one another?

It's easy to show love to those who gave us love and kindness, and less so to those who were unkind or absent. The best way to heal any difficulties is to try to set aside personal feelings. Those feelings themselves could be the tears of rage that blind clear sight.

Kristina attended one of our ancestral healing retreats and it was apparent her father's ancestors were very present in spirit at the retreat. She then told us she hadn't seen them for years and was no longer in contact with her father. During the retreat, I suggested she visit her paternal parents' grave on her way home and think about calling on her father to see if she could address some of her emotional pain from childhood. Here's what she said:

### Kristina's story

*My parents divorced when I was 14 years old. My sister and I saw our father only two or three times afterwards.*

*I'm now married with three children. After attending the ancestral retreat, I realized it was important to connect with my father's family and my ancestors in general. I'd completely blanked them out. Not even my children knew about them. I'd effectively erased my father and his side of the family from our family story, deleting the past.*

*One day, when my son was six years old, I decided to paint the wall around the fireplace and we hung some family photographs, including some from my father's side. Afterwards, he asked questions about who was in them. It was only then I realized that although my mother had remarried, I'd never told the children my stepfather wasn't their real grandfather. To avoid this potentially only coming to light many years later at his funeral, I decided to explain to the children who my real father was and we arranged a visit.*

*As soon as we arrived at his house, it all came back to me. It was ghastly. He was rude, critical and ignored the presence of my daughters in favour of my son. Nothing they could do was without criticism. Whether they were eating, standing, sitting, whatever, he continually put them down. As this was the first time he'd met the children, it shocked me, as they'd been so well behaved. He hadn't changed his behaviour at all since I'd last seen him.*

*The journey home was spent in silence as we each reflected on the experience. I thanked them for behaving so well and my daughter said, 'Poor you, Mummy. Was he always like that?'*

*On the way home, we took a detour to visit my paternal grandparents' grave. The children were so quiet and peaceful as we busied ourselves tidying the gravestones and pulling out the weeds. It was then that I felt the spirit of my paternal grandmother, who had always said she wanted to dance at my wedding. She thanked me for bringing the children, and I could feel her unconditional love and connection with us. I realized then that if we hadn't gone to see my father, we'd never have reconciled our connection with his side of the family. I felt I'd done my duty both to him and my children, who now knew who he was and of his existence.*

*We received a call that he'd passed away five years later. No one knew he was unwell and it was a shock to hear he'd died, but I felt I'd reconciled my relationship with him during that visit. I felt at peace and knew his deceased parents would be with him.*

If this has happened in your life, the first thing is to be kind to yourself. Realize that what transpired in your childhood was *not* your fault. It might be hard to feel forgiveness for what happened to you when you were growing up, but it's an important step when it comes to moving on and healing. Otherwise, the only thing you'll have achieved is passing on and reflecting the same issues your family learned and inherited.

If you can identify these influences, they can have tremendous value in terms of gaining a deeper understanding of yourself. It would be impossible to free yourself from all of your childhood conditioning, but you can learn to accept what you cannot change and focus instead on what you can. This is what ancestral healing is all about.

Start with a small daily prayer, simply asking to be held in love by the good and loving ancestors. This is a great place to start. From here, be grateful for the little things in your life. For those friends who are there when you really need them, and for the family you do have.

## Birth and children

When we're conceived, the time spent in our mother's womb teaches us about our family. We learn about their circumstances and their lives, preparing us for the place we find ourselves in once we're born. This is when our family shadows begin to touch us. It's in the womb that we encounter our father's attitude to our arrival and his feelings towards us. It's here that we learn how much we're wanted. Gradually, we take on the shadow of our parents' relationship and the memories of our own parents' conception, birth and so on.

Inga is a yoga teacher and when she was pregnant with her son, she started to have some irrational thoughts that she was going to die during childbirth:

### Inga's story

*Before the birth of our first son, I was really, really afraid. It was like a fog of fear, this sense of foreboding that something bad would happen. When I dug really deep, I realized it was because I believed I wouldn't survive the birth. I was super afraid of going to hospital, believing they'd do things to me that I didn't want and that they'd somehow sacrifice me to save the baby. Perhaps cut me open to make sure the baby lived. I couldn't understand why I felt this way and it made no sense whatsoever. It was hard to talk to anyone about it either, because everyone confirmed what my rational mind already knew: that it wasn't going to happen.*

*I went to a drumming workshop and had this vision in which a man appeared to me. I believe it was my great-grandfather and he took me down to the basement of a hospital to show me what had happened to his wife. I could see how her life had been sacrificed at the birth of her child, during which something had happened, whereby they'd chosen to let her die and the baby live. I saw how she'd been cut open and then sewn together again. On my way back home, they both came to me on the ferry and I could see there was a lot of trauma still there.*

*The moment I saw this past event, the fear that I'd inherited from several generations back made sense. It was like the last piece of the puzzle had been put in place and with this knowledge, it helped me to release the fear completely. Since then, I've been looking into my family tree, trying to find out who they are, all the way back to the mid-1800s. I've freed a lot of my uncertainties and understood they've come from my ancestors. I can see how they seeped down from my grandma, through my mum, and almost certainly even several generations before that.*

The purpose of your personal ancestral healing journey is to find ways to look at your own ancestral inheritance so you may embark on a voyage of self-discovery to connect with your ancestral roots. The journey begins with an exploration of your family's history, but it's important to discover your own first, from the time of your conception right through to the present day. Details surrounding how you were brought up and how your parents, caregivers and extended family responded to you from birth onwards has a significant influence on your self-esteem, mental health and emotional wellbeing.

## Voyage of self-discovery

If you know what transpired at your conception, discovering what was happening in your parents' lives at the time, what the political and historical climate was, where they were living and who with, will give you a sense of what was occurring both when you were conceived and while you were in your mother's womb.

- Start by placing a photograph of yourself as a baby on your ancestral altar and light a candle. If you don't have one, then a family memento or a photograph of your parents around the time of your birth would suffice.
- If you want to address your own children's conception, place their photographs on the altar – reflect on how both you and your partner felt at that time and about their conception in general.
- Write in your journal what you remember of their birth and post-birth, paying particular attention to how you felt about your child.
- Turn your attention to your child's response and reactions to you as their carer and write down any thoughts that come to you.
- Reflect on what you'd have done differently for them if you had your time again.
- Once you've completed the exercise, say a prayer for the memory of the conception and if it held any trauma or dysfunction, ask for it to be released.

---

## Mothers

Our mother is our primary relationship and their imprint on us is intrinsic. We're literally a part of them and they're a part of us. The emotional implications of a 'good' or 'bad' mother are indelibly linked with aeons of ancestral expectation and conditioning. For daughters, their mother is their first role model and they mould themselves to her image even when her example is an unhealthy one. For sons, their relationship with their mother is their first connection. It's she who sets the example on how to behave or act within their own future relationships.

As a mother myself (Natalia), I realize many of us try to be all things to all people. We take on too much, we hide our true feelings and we struggle to find the boundaries between being open and giving while being conscious that we must take care of ourselves, too.

When a mother holds her child in her arms for the first time, she feels many emotions. As they're growing up, she can feel every wave of every emotion ever felt, from love to hate and back to love. However, as all of us have been mothered ourselves, both good and bad ideas of mothering will be passed down to our children. We can celebrate the best versions of our mothers and heal the rest by being aware that we can change what's been handed to us as children. The cure in all cases is love – deep, unconditional loving.

In ancient and traditional cultures, fertility was one of the prime gifts we hoped to receive from our ancestors. They were the ones who would gift us a child from the spirit realms. Infertility was sometimes seen as a curse or a sign of displeasure in ancestral spheres. However, the extended family did much to mitigate the personal loss.

In Hawaii, a sense of family doesn't just rely on blood ties. Children are loved and esteemed whatever the circumstances of their birth. When one woman cannot conceive, another will gift her a child. Today, Western rules around adoption aren't easy and when the adopted child joins another family, this is a part of the gifting of children through family systems. Traditional cultures keep the community intact and spread the love throughout all family lineages, including through surrogacy and adoption. In Olena's case, her infertility was treated in Eastern Europe through an egg donor. She and her partner now have a daughter:

**Olena's story**

*When I was pregnant, I did some work around fear as I could feel it welling up inside me. I knew it wasn't my own fears I was experiencing. It was from being inside my mother's womb and the fear she felt at the time. Once my daughter was born, it took months to bond and feel I could give all of my heart and love to her, as there was an overwhelming sense that she could die at any time.*

*It took some deep work to discover that when I was in my mother's womb, I brought with me all of the souls of our family line from babies who were stillborn or who died shortly after birth. They carried with them all the grief from their mothers who came before me. Afterwards, the sense of suffocation I felt around the fear that my daughter would die passed. Coming from a Catholic family where religion played an important part,*

*I was able to honour these souls on an Imbolc retreat celebrating the beginning of spring when sitting in a church one day. It was during this celebration that they were released to the light and found peace.*

*One of my grandmothers had seven children and the other had 15, all of whom survived. There was never any talk about how they struggled as women and mothers. It was only after becoming one myself that I found I could fully appreciate and connect with what they went through, including the sacrifices they made for their children and how this affected their wellbeing.*

*Maintaining cultural identity was important to my family, as leaving native Eastern European countries and settling in Canada happened in living memory. Of all of the grandchildren, and even many of the children of my grandparents, I was one of the most involved when it came to following traditions and could literally feel myself being pulled back by the ancestors. It might seem strange, but even after moving to Europe, I've never been to my family's native countries, but with the transition to motherhood, I feel the time is coming. Because my daughter was conceived using egg donor IVF in the Czech Republic, I feel it's essential to understand the influences of this family line on her and her life and for her to connect to that as she gets older.*

## Fathers

The father of the family is an important figure whether he's present, absent or unknown. He's always going to be our father whether we have a relationship with him or not. Fatherhood has changed considerably over the past 20 years, with more fathers playing a central role in parenting. Even the gender gap between parental roles has shortened. This isn't the case in all cultures, where the role of the father and mother within the family unit remains the same as it has been for generations.

Terry believes his ideal of becoming a father was so different to that of his own father:

> *My father was an archetypal man from his generation who had just come out of the Royal Navy after the Second World War ended. He then went into the fire service working shifts and from time to time he took on a second job just to pay the bills. He was pretty absent during my childhood, so when I became a father, I had to learn to do it differently. My father never attended my birth, but I was there at the birth of all of our children. I was a hands-on dad to our three children and was fortunate to work from home.*

Compassion and forgiveness can prevent a repeat of the same cycles of dysfunctional behaviour. Sometimes it's the case that the stepfather or adoptive father becomes the best father figure we could have, and it's their love and support that changes the dynamic within the family from negative to positive in its legacy despite the absence of bloodlines.

This is the case in Fredrich's life, where he changed his family history by becoming a different example of a father to that of his own experience of fatherhood as a boy:

**Fredrich's story**

*I haven't traced my father's line, but I do know that my paternal grandfather never went near his wife again after she conceived my father. My father had a very difficult relationship with his parents, and both my father and grandfather have narcissistic personality disorders. Some people who don't have or want children could be influenced by the past in their decision, which is the unconscious, unhealed wounding in their ancestral history at work. I've done my very best to be conscious of my ancestral inheritance and my own emotions in order to be a good, connected, respectful and loving father to my own sons.*

Just as infertility or the decision not to have children can be rooted in inherited patterns, trauma such as the loss of a parent during childhood can cause people to struggle with becoming a parent themselves. We've witnessed many times the deep sadness of clients who have lost their parents before they had children of their own, or who were unable to have children or who made a choice not to have them. To change this, first they must learn to accept themselves and how life has been for them, as part of the healing process is acceptance of what's happened. Sometimes this calls for forgiveness and even cutting ties to release the sadness so that they might heal. Men often have uncertain feelings about having children and dealing with fatherhood, which could come from this ancestral lineage of difficult and unloving fathers. The idea that to be a father could cause a repeat of past issues or that they're unable to be a good father makes the decision to become one difficult at times.

Letting go of thinking about how they want to be as a father changes the legacy for their own children.

## Cutting the cord

We're all connected by what essentially amounts to an invisible umbilical cord, which extends from the eldest ancestor to the youngest and to those who have yet to be born. If you imagine this cord as being a string of prayer beads, you'll see that it connects us to the beginning, no matter how distant, and that this connection has always been a continuum.

As we address the family inheritance, we realize families are complex. We're all born to one, whether we know, like or are accepted by individual members or not. We're individually original from each other, for we share both a sense of similarity and in certain cases, extreme differences. We're a part of them and they're a part of us. As such, we cannot fully address our ancestral healing without acknowledging our relationships with our family.

When addressing your family dynamics, you should begin by not only recollecting times when you were rejected, disappointed, hurt or left feeling powerless, but also the instances when you were accepted and loved. The purpose of these memories is to gain clarity on how you were affected, as well as what makes you feel insecure and unloved and by whom, and also when you felt loved and valued.

It's at these times that we recognize our family sometimes isn't enough. It's only as adults that we accept what exists in our own families by learning to adapt and to accept what we cannot change. These issues almost always begin in early childhood, rooted in the relationships we have with our parents and siblings.

Many of us have suffered because of difficult, challenging relationships with someone from our childhood owing to the decisions made for us by parents, primary caregivers and even grandparents. This next exercise will help you to come to terms with difficult family relationships. It's particularly useful when you still have negative feelings about a family member or there's been a long-term estrangement that hasn't been dealt with, expressed or healed.

## Cutting ties

Before you begin, write down the answers to these questions:

1. Who do you want to forgive?
2. Who's hurt you, when and why?
3. When did it begin?

Making the decision to let go is the first step to your ancestral healing.

- First, light a candle at your ancestral altar.
- Ask that the wise and compassionate ancestors help you to let go of your past wounds and hurts.
- Open your heart and ask the same of the person who's hurt you, so they, too, can let go.
- Write down what you wish to say to the person and as you are doing this, let any thoughts or feelings of anger, hurt or rage find their way onto the page.
- When you've finished, don't read what you've written.
- Take the piece of paper, fold it up and burn it in the flame of a candle or open fire.
- Watch it burn away symbolically in the flames.
- Say to yourself *'I am now free of this hurt and pain. I release it to the ancestors for their help to heal past struggles in my relationship with (name).'*

- For the next step, repeat the above saying, either out loud or in your mind, until you're ready to forgive and let go of the past.
- If you still feel an emotional tie, then repeat this process a few days later and when doing so, go deeper into your heart to let go.
- Look at your attachments to your anger or hurt and consider why you're still unable to forgive them.
- When you repeat the ritual, say out loud or silently to yourself three times *'I am now free of this inherited pain and heartbreak. I release it to the ancestors, for it is now theirs to deal with, so I can move on and be at peace.'*

If you find it too difficult to let go of the unreconciled feelings of what happened between you and the family member who hurt you, then maybe it's time to look back at the work you've done on your ancestral healing and continue this process on your own. However, this could be a good moment to think about seeking advice and support from a professional therapist who specializes in family issues. It's important to reconcile your own personal feelings about your relationship with certain people. While we cannot change others, we can change ourselves.

You need to know what you truly want from the process of letting go. Spend time with your journal each week, looking back at everything you've become aware of. Consider what you're happy to accept and what issues you'd prefer to lose.

---

To work on your ancestral healing, you must have faith and determination to be free of all that makes you unhappy and unwell from your ancestral family history. The release of our loved ones and those who are no longer alive has a profound effect on us and to be able to make changes, we need to look back at their lives before we can fully heal our own.

Deciding what aspects of your inheritance you'd like to change will take time. Be honest and realistic about what you can change and what you cannot. Changing your relationship with your living family is part of this process. Go back through the emotional and psychological issues you've uncovered so far, write down a list of positive and negative traits you've inherited and finally, note what you'd like to heal or change about your family's attitudes and beliefs.

Before you embark on discovering your family stories and making changes, conduct a ritual to celebrate your rebirth. This could be a simple act of going to your favourite place and writing a letter to your ancestors telling them what you want to heal and what steps you're taking in your family's ancestral healing journey. Bury the letter in the earth and plant a tree above it as a gift of rebirth both for yourself and for your ancestors.

Create some baby steps in your daily life to help manage the process of empowering the positive. Take the best of what you've inherited from your family while releasing and letting go of the negative influences that no longer serve you.

Chapter 2

# Discovering Your Family Tree

*'History remembers only the celebrated, genealogy remembers them all.'*

LAURENCE OVERMIRE

When you search among the branches of your family tree, excavating your family history and revealing lost and forgotten family members, you can discover the reasons why you may need to address your family heritage. You may even pull out a leading thread and change things for the better, by understanding how the various interfaces and interlacing of their family stories could all unravel the history of your own family and shed perspective on the human continuum.

By observing connections between different family members, you may find out about family secrets. You may learn why you've inherited certain behaviours, including some that haven't been discussed in the past. You may discover people in your family who have felt dislocated or alienated from their heritage but resisted learning about it. Or those who have searched tirelessly to find that thread that connects them to the family tree may reveal themselves. Furthermore, by knowing the roots of your heritage and finding pathways to your relatives, it can give you a sense of belonging, which may impact on future generations.

Not everyone who traces their family history is searching to address inherited problems or wanting to start to process their ancestral healing. There are many wide-ranging reasons for taking an interest in tracing family heritage, such as becoming or losing a parent, uncovering a hidden adoption, investigating inherited physical or mental illnesses that have afflicted more than one generation, or simply the desire to know where your family came from.

During this process, it can be immensely healing to return to the country of origin of your family roots and restore a sense of belonging. It's then that family stories become clearer as the reasons for their passions, interests and hobbies acquire context and so on.

Sarah began tracing her family history after her father died, when she was left some documents about her mother's family:

### Sarah's story

*Having known remarkably little about my mother's family, as she died when I was five, I went on a quest to find out more in my 40s. I discovered her father's family were all from Scotland. I took my family up there and found the church where my great-grandfather was minister for over 40 years. I also saw the house my grandfather grew up in – where his mother died after giving birth to his triplet sisters.*

*One sister died as a child and the other two went on to become amazing sportswomen in their day, playing hockey and cricket for Scotland. It was remarkable to discover all this and I found I was able to feel their presence and still do. There's a realization now that they're part of my children and me. Regardless of what went on in their lives, I have a natural feeling of respect for them. Remembering them gave me a tremendous sense of peace and even re-connection. They all seem so familiar to me now, whereas before there was nothing.*

## Ancestry and family history research

Researching relevant aspects or sectors of history can put past family events in context and give you a sense of how they might have affected your ancestors at the time, providing an indication of how they can still be felt in your family's lives today.

### *Getting started*

A bit of planning and preparation will save you a lot of wasted time and money. Don't believe rumours, hearsay or family traditions and stories about your family, even from family members, until you've checked all the details thoroughly.

Simple planning and fact-finding can start with living relatives: your parents, grandparents, uncles, aunts. Ask them what they know of their parents. Establish good research skills from the start, hence the reason for starting backwards with your most recent known ancestors (parents, then grandparents, then further back). This will establish your recent lineage, which can then be backed up by obtaining birth, marriage and death certificates from the General Registry Office (GRO). Afterwards, you can obtain further details from census returns, which will back up what you've already discovered.

### *Using census records*

The earliest full census records start in 1841 and are conducted every 10 years but only published once every 100 years. Earlier census records start from 1801 but list populations in a more random way. Each successive one gives more detail than the previous. The 1911 census, for example, records the number of children the wife of the head of the household gave birth to and the number still living. The woman can often be deemed the head of the household, especially if she's a widow or her husband is away with one of the armed services on the day the census was taken.

Typically, the information on a census will include, in addition to the head of the household and spouse, all living children at the time of the visit, any other family members, their relation to the head of the household and any other occupants, such as lodgers. Details such as their ages, occupation, illnesses, disabilities and where they were born are recorded. A census record can be useful to corroborate what you've found on a birth, marriage or death certificate.

## *Family trees*

Using information and details from your research into your family history combined with what you know of your family will give you enough information to draw up a basic family tree. There are several family trees you can use, depending on how much detail and how far back a pedigree you want to create. Basic outlines of family trees can usually be found for free on the Internet if you search Google Images, or you can create one yourself using Microsoft Word tables and charts. PowerPoint is another useful resource enabling you to incorporate one generation per slide. If you subscribe to a family history database such as Genes Reunited, access is granted enabling you to form your family tree using their software, whereby you can insert boxes for each family member as you go along.

In the main, the male parent is always listed on the left of the family tree and the female on the right.

1. In the case of ambiguity, assume a male-female relationship, rather than a male-male or female-female one.

2. A spouse must always be closer to his/her first partner, then the second partner (if any) and so on.
3. The eldest child is always depicted on the left of his/her family, the youngest on the right.

### *Types of family tree*

There are many types of family tree sequences and you can always check online to see which would suit your family tree or requirements best. Perhaps the most familiar family tree is the drop-line chart, which you may have seen on TV programmes such as *Who Do You Think You Are?*

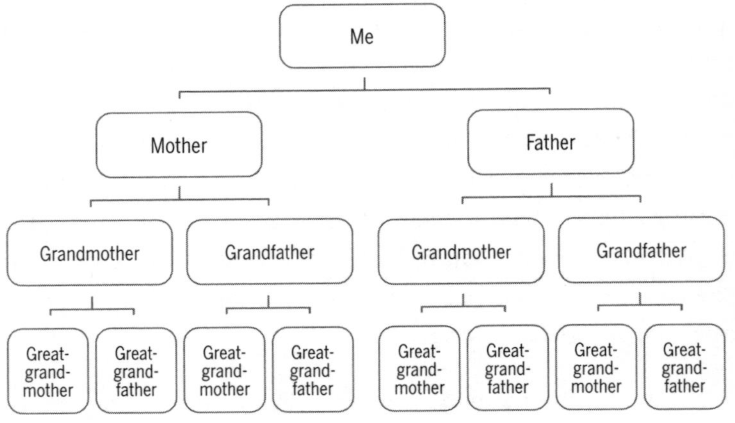


*Drop-line chart*

As you will see from the image, this example is actually the other way round, with the female lineage on the left and the male on the right. This is fine as long as you remember which is which and it's made clear.

Other charts include the pedigree chart, which shows relationships between family members. Other forms of this chart can be used to show genetic representations, such as the inheritance of diseases or traits through generations.

There's also the concentric tree:

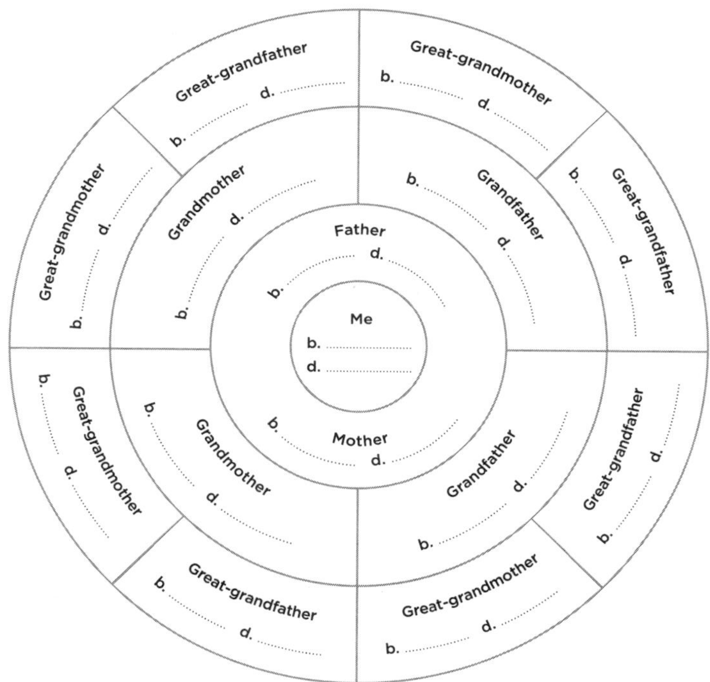


*Concentric tree chart*

There are variations, but usually yourself and your spouse's details are placed at the centre, working outwards.

And there are more elaborate designs like these:

*Decorative tree designs*

Family tree templates can be found on the Internet, or for more detailed ones, try www.ancestry.com and www.genesreunited.co.uk.

Other genealogical publishers and guides include Burke's Peerage and Debrett's Peerage, which traces information about the royal family and peerage, both of which use the Narrative Indented Tree, allowing for several children and their descendants to be included. Each generation is assigned a number or letter. The children of a couple are then listed, with any marriages and subsequent children indented. It's not the easiest to navigate and is generally unsuitable if you just want to record ancestors going back a couple of generations. Please note that Burke's Peerage and Debrett's Peerage are no longer published every year because of the research involved, but the latter is published every four years with yearly online updates.[4]

### Messaging boards

Databases such as Ancestry or Genes Reunited offer this service. This platform enables you to contact other people who have uploaded a family tree that includes some of your ancestors and they may grant you access to their family tree. If you locate that missing, elusive ancestor, take care to check the details marry up with what you've discovered rather than it just being someone with a similar name to one of your ancestors. There are forums where you can ask a question about your family and then wait for answers to be posted from respondents who may or may not be closely related to you. Be prepared, though, to answer questions about your own family tree – the question-and-answer forum works both ways.

### DNA testing

Many sites such as Ancestry and MyHeritage offer DNA testing kits, which aren't as expensive as they might sound. Each company has a different slant on what they offer, so choose carefully. First, find out if a sibling or relative has done this already, as the results will likely be identical, but even first cousins may have different results. DNA testing has become popular and DNA kits can yield surprising results.

## Discovering your family history

Family stories connect the names in the family tree, making their lives real. For example, you might discover someone extraordinary in the family, such as the first person to achieve something exceptional in medicine or politics, or a father and son who made a fortune, or a relative who lost everything and went to the workhouse. These people may well have changed the legacy they left their descendants while surviving challenges in their lives. In excavating the history of some of your ancestors, you'll see how they changed the lives of those who came after them and before you.

Researching family history makes sense of the stories that have been rumoured or forgotten or of silenced memories. At the beginning of the 20th century, families were often close geographically. Grandparents lived nearby who would tell stories about what life was like then, and about family dramas and scandals. Over the last century or two, families have moved away from each other, even changing continents to find a new destiny, or to escape war, persecution or famine. Sometimes it might have been that a bigamous marriage or illegitimate child prompted a move. In Europe, the last 250 years alone have brought revolution, two world wars, bitter civil wars, genocide and occupation.

Generally, our ancestors were primarily concerned with the daily struggle to survive and the focus of their lives was within the local community in which they resided. Only a few of our ancestors were preoccupied with national issues, as many were illiterate. In England, the countrywide Elementary Education Act was set up in 1870, with just 60 per cent of men and 40 per cent of women being literate at the time. For the majority, life revolved around the home, the Church, religious places of worship, schools if they were available, the workplace and social recreational places such as public houses.

## Historical family research

To begin, it can be useful to write down everything you discover through your research and there are helpful guidelines when setting out on this historical journey. Record everything (much easier these days with online access and websites) and collect as much information as possible from photographs, documents and family stories. Someone else in your family may have started down the genealogy path before you. It's relatively easy to track down your ancestors on the civil registration and census documents from the middle of 1800s onwards given online resources. Even before that, parish records can be viewed as far back as 1537. The further back you go, the harder it becomes, but it's not impossible.

Family patterns of births, deaths, occupations, migrations, persecution, famine, sickness, mortality and ambitions of family members during peacetime, wartime, civil war and times of great change may become obvious. Each nation had its own specific traumas and times of great wealth and poverty. And each century had its own preoccupations. All of these historical events affected your family personally, nationally and internationally, forming part of the family stories. It's like being a detective, piecing together how they relate to inherited illnesses and behaviours, cultural views, religious beliefs and so on. Finding out about characteristics, talents and passions can be enlightening, as Julia discovered, having always been interested in her family history:

**Julia's story**

*I first encountered my family tree when my splendid great-aunt held an 80th birthday party, to which she invited several cousins from branches I'd never heard of. At the time, she handed out copies of the family tree she'd carefully researched in a trio of Essex villages, going back centuries. The most intriguing story was of two sisters marrying two brothers in the 1870s, then two deaths leading to the survivors marrying each other. Could I even imagine being a woman who went through that? Sometime later, her deed of probate emerged from my father's safe and I saw I'd given my daughter her name.*

*As I spent time delving, the tree got larger and older. A Huguenot ancestor brought artistic and musical genes to the family on one side, in which records revealed that an Isabelle - a Huguenot born in Picardy - married in London in 1686, leading to generations of professional artists and musicians, both men and women. A travelling violinist of the 18th century obviously had them on the other side, too. My children both resonate with music, though very differently, so I was excited to find it running back so far through the family tree.*

Can you find patterns of birth, death, sickness and mortality in your family? How about against a national story of war and peace, prosperity and hardship? Can you find a skeleton in the lives of family members to fill in on your family tree during periods of growth and decline, abrupt change or peaceful continuity?

## Where do you connect with the family story?

When we find out where we come from - as in our DNA, ethnicity, family history and culture - we come to recognize both the wonderful and the terrible about our family. This knowledge can help us to discover more about who we are and is a powerful tool to heal our wounds and those of our family.

If you detect a family pattern or ancestral behavioural issues that need to be addressed, make a note and return to the issues one at a time to discover if there are any negative, difficult or violent characters linked to these specific concerns. Start by searching through the family stories. If you're adopted or don't have any information about your family, consider DNA testing. If you discover living family members or come across family ancestral stories, document what you find in a journal. If you want, you can address both your adoptive and your biological family stories.

The process of exploring family history can help to bring deeper understanding. It can allow you to realize previously unexpressed aspects of yourself, such as current life choices that may not be right for you. Or you may identify certain relationships and friendships that aren't suitable or supportive. New talents and ambitions may lie dormant, including spiritual ones. As we learn about our history, we ignite the creativity and connection we have with the many ancestors who walked before we existed.

Having uncovered some of your history, you can review your family in light of the tree. Consider how some of the lives and deaths of your ancestral family align with current behaviours, beliefs, anxiety disorders, creative impulses or gifts. See if you can uncover personality traits appearing regularly in your family. Do you come from a family of stubborn, impatient or angry people who frequently make unfortunate decisions or forge dubious relationships? Or perhaps you're from a family who are affectionate and generous. Evaluate what you've exposed in a neutral way as if watching from the outside. Which qualities could be useful? Which can be managed and what can be healed?

Samantha is from Yorkshire and when her house was healed by Terry, she discovered a family secret of her own:

### Samantha's story

*When Terry came to do a house clearing for us, he was totally taken by a portrait of my great-grandmother, Alice. He said I needed to find out more about her as he felt something was going on there. Over time, I discovered she'd married a titled man in Ireland, many years her senior, who, by all accounts, was powerful and brutal. She had several children with him but then ran off with the 'land agent' and set up a new life in Paris, where she had another child. Because she left her children, she became a shamed woman, to the point where the story tells of her portrait being turned to face the wall in the dining hall. She was later ditched by the 'land agent' and returned to England. I now realize how this trauma could have a direct impact on my confidence and trust when it comes to going about life.*

## Haunted families

When you embark on unravelling your family stories, you begin to think of them as real people, which is when you start to consider how you feel about your own family history. We might have considered our family's past, but until something happens, or you're given a legacy or you come across a family story, you will invariably fail to see the patterns and how these stories relate to you and who you are today.

Lisa is a friend of ours who lives in Arizona and whose family originated from Utah, USA. She's always been interested in finding out more about her family heritage, as she felt she was somehow haunted or cursed. She had a strong perception that negative family history was affecting her today. Typical indicators are not feeling yourself, low moods that come on for no reason and a strange sense of carrying a burden that you know isn't yours. These types of hauntings can be felt as familiar family characteristics or quirks, which is exactly what Lisa discovered:

### Lisa's story

*After a lifetime of moaning to anyone who would listen that I felt like I was cursed (even though I didn't believe in curses at the time), I came across something revealing while conducting genealogy research. I finally discovered that there was indeed a curse cast long ago on one of my ancestors' families in the midst of a well-documented witch trial in 1677, in which a woman was burned at the stake after being accused of witchcraft by one of my ancestors. Documentation stated that she cast a generational curse on him and his descendants.*

*In modern times, we tend to believe those poor unfortunate souls back then were innocent of the witchcraft of which they were accused, and most were – I actually believe the woman in my family's story was innocent. But then how can anyone being burned at the stake for a crime they didn't commit not send enraged, vengeful energy towards those who caused her unjust torture? Whether she intended to blast them with a curse or not, how could she not? There must be ripples of horror still cascading through the generations – a nightmarish butterfly effect.*

*If the family believed there was a curse, then surely they'd act accordingly, changing their behaviours and the situations they attracted to themselves. Owing to feelings of guilt after watching her execution, they might even subconsciously torture themselves with self-fulfilling prophecies of punishment. Eventually, the story of the curse would no longer be passed down through the generations, but the inherited behaviours and negative attractions would remain set in place until someone uncovered them and exposed them to the light of day. I feel like that's my role in the story – simply because it's now been exposed. And now I know about it, I feel obliged to unearth what happened and find some way to soothe the horrific energy patterns that were put into play hundreds of years ago.*

*While researching further, I've found numerous incidents in that particular branch of my family tree involving pain or death by burning. Almost 100 years ago, three of my ancestors were killed in a coalmine explosion. The next generation down, another ancestor died because of a kitchen fire. Another generation younger, an ancestor's house burned down and an uncle became chief of the local fire department. Yet another ancestor was diagnosed with lung cancer from smoking and suffered acute side effects from the burning of the radiation therapy.*

*I'm convinced these events are all connected and I'm doing everything I know to heal the energetic rift. I recently travelled to the site of the execution to offer prayers of apology and to ask for forgiveness. Since then, my luck and my health have improved. My head is clearer and I feel lighter. I no longer feel tortured by a free-floating sense of anxiety that I've done something horrible. It's my hope that this is the end of the story and that all of the affected souls are now free from the repercussions of a mistake made centuries ago.*

## Discovering your family's heritage

When you've done your research, list the maternal side as far back as you can go with the information you have, then do the same with the paternal side. Some people have researched back to the 10th century and found 1,200 people in their family tree, but as there is less and less information the further back you go, generally family traits can only be determined for three or four generations. For now, just work back over four generations, so you can fill in those details that will give you enough information about your inheritance. It's common for most families to be able to research back three to six generations and occasionally much further.

When writing out your family tree, list details such as: births (including any known dates), country of birth, cultural and religious influences, marriages and to whom, illnesses (including mental and physical illness), typical family traits and characteristics, deaths. These lists should comprise uncles, aunts, great-aunts and -uncles, any siblings, including adopted or extended family members.

List:

- status and financial issues
- family secrets
- controlling personalities
- sexual issues
- suicides
- murderous tendencies
- criminal propensities

- illegitimacy
- accidental deaths
- any known abuse
- traumatic deaths

Now list any positive talents:

- musical and artistic flairs
- financial gains, rewards and good deeds
- sporting successes
- educational learnings and qualifications gained
- community welfare projects engaged in
- creative and pioneering achievements
- charitable donations and contributions, not just financial

In your own opinion, conclude with the strengths and weaknesses of each family member from the research conducted. List influences and consider which ones are positive and negative. What do you believe is the legacy for your family for future generations? Consider their talents, gifts and traits.

**You could go deeper by asking further questions of your family history:**

- What is the education trajectory of your family?
- How has it changed across the generations?

- Do you notice any changes across time in terms of the distances between the birth places of the couples?
- What social, cultural or political challenges have different generations faced?
- Can you identify any changes or transitions that may have occurred owing to these challenges?
- How do you think your family history and relationships may have impacted on how you understand your own identity?

---

The more information you can uncover, the better, as it can be helpful in consolidating a legacy that future generations can build upon.

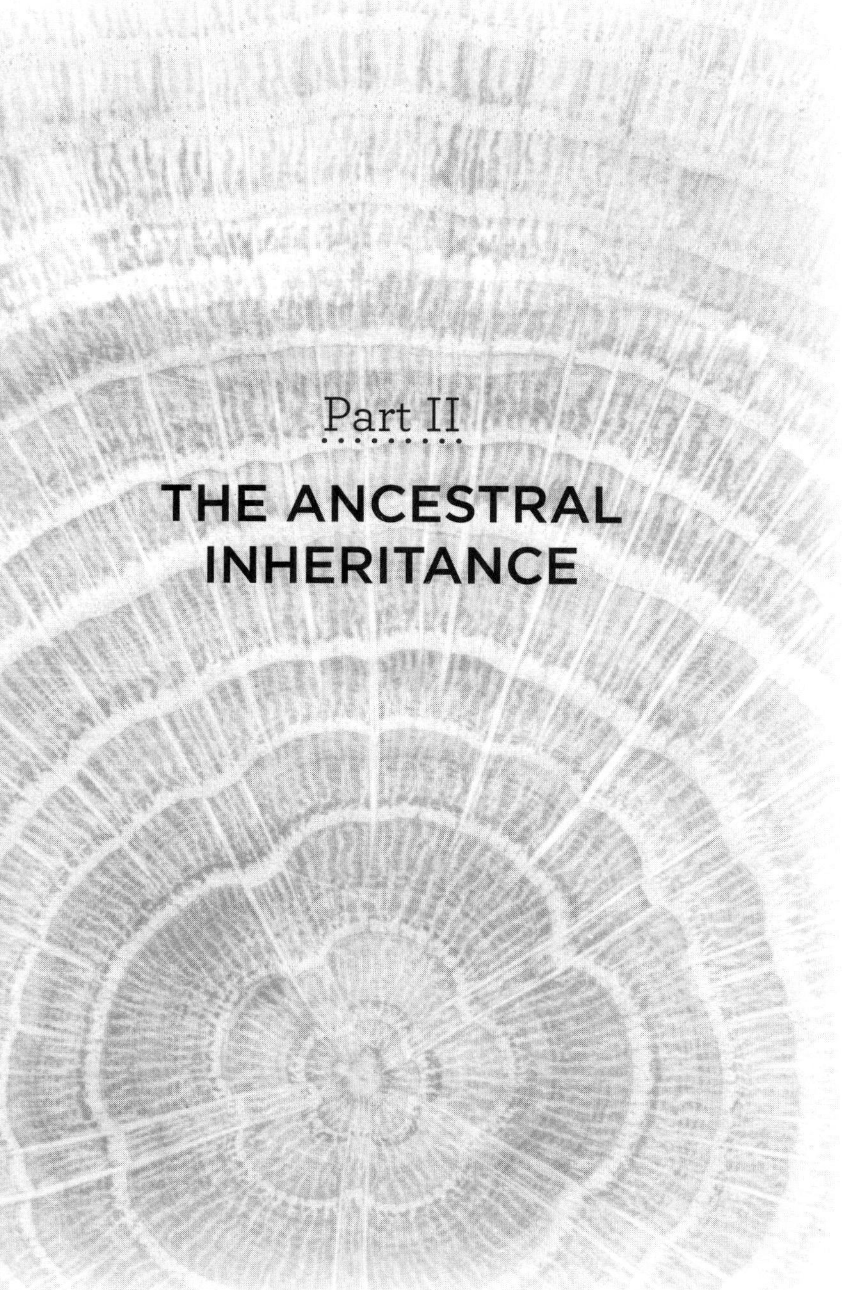

# Part II

# THE ANCESTRAL INHERITANCE

## Chapter 3

# Your Biological Inheritance

*'Biological inheritance may be a reality, but it doesn't have to be our destiny.'*

MARK WOLYNN

Where do we come from? How often have you asked yourself that question? You may know your parents, even your grandparents, but often most of us don't know anything far beyond that. For most of us, the trail begins to disappear early down the family tree, but each of us still carries a root of where we came from within the stories from our ancestors in every cell of our body, in our DNA. This molecule holds the instructions for growth and development in every living being and is how genetic material is handed down from generation to generation. An example of the complexities of our biological heritage is the fact that if we go back 13 generations, we have at least 30,000 direct ancestors. Therefore, it means that within our DNA, we carry not only our history, but also the history of the human race.

What we personally inherit is a combination of our biological and emotional traits individually selected by nature and chosen from our family heritage. We carry these predispositions in our genes, affected by cultural elements as well as the capacities and constraints of those we've been born to. Human development is a two-way transitional impact, influenced not only by our upbringing and environment, but also by the fact that we're actively able to influence it ourselves. Nothing is static and nothing remains the same - fluidity and change run through the inheritance of all families.

However, as we start to address our biological inheritance (nature) and our social cultural environment (nurture), we realize we have our own unique perspective of the world, as well as some of the abilities and limitations of those we've been born through. As we grow and expand our perspective, we discover how to utilize the different skills we need to help us manage our biological, social and psychological influences.

The origin of certain inherited illnesses may be difficult to locate, but searching out the roots of dysfunction gives us a sense of awareness at the very least. At last, scientific studies are now finding more evidence to suggest that if we can do anything to prevent or change the inherited messages from our ancestors, it's to understand how biological heredities are stored and transmitted between generations.

Jose Stevens, president and co-founder of Power Path Seminars, discusses this understanding in *The Three Ancestral Threads and How They Affect Your Present Life*.[5] He explained that some indigenous peoples - especially South Pacific indigenous cultures and other cultures in that part of the world - have an excellent understanding of how patterns are stored in the hard tissues of the body. The oldest patterns that go back a long time are stored in the hardest tissues of the body, which are the bones and the teeth. The next layer is the cartilage, which is softer than bone but still harder than tissue. The most recent patterns are stored in the soft tissues of the body, meaning that they don't go back as far. All patterns are stored in the physical body but can be transmitted to the personality. Each individual has a male side and a female side, and may store both male and female patterns in their bones, perhaps even exhibiting some of those behaviours themselves. This topic is complex, but to give an example, if all males in one family were heavy drinkers and unsupportive towards their families, and the females were long-suffering victims of that behaviour, future family members might exhibit those same behaviours regardless of their gender. In other words, they inherit those propensities on the male side.

## Genetics

Paul Berg, co-inventor of genetic engineering, said, 'All disease is genetic.'[6] This would suggest our genetic inheritance is more prominent than environmental influences.

It would mean our biological responses and some genes are activated by both external triggers and the effect of random social situations that can affect biological development. For instance, a mutant BRCA1 gene increases the risk of breast cancer, but not all women carrying the BRCA1 mutation develop cancer. So even if a gene is inherited, its capacity to make an actual attribute in a person isn't absolute. Some women will develop aggressive cancer in their 30s, while others will develop a less aggressive cancer in their 50s and some who carry the BRCA1 may never develop it.

Passing on genetic information to the next generation is a matter of chance. Parents are proud to pass on their good looks, blue eyes or sports prowess but feel devastated when it might be something dangerous. For example, a heart condition such as hypertrophic cardiomyopathy, which can cause the heart to enlarge with risk of heart failure or sudden death, or the presence of gene variants that increase the risk of the young having breast or bowel cancer. Family legacy can be a source not only of pride, but also sadness, pain and fear.

Genetic disorders can be the result of abnormalities such as gene mutation or additional chromosomes. The effects of abnormalities in an individual's DNA were once entirely unpredictable. However, modern medicine has produced methods of identifying the potential health outcomes of genetic disorders. Professionals such as Janice Bailey, a specialist nurse from Somerset, can now identify some of the current best practices for detecting, treating and potentially preventing some genetic disorders:

### Janice's story

*The human genome – 'the recipe for us' – is so mind-bogglingly large. If one were to speak one letter of DNA per second for 24 hours a day, it would take 100 years to recite the whole human genome. With approximately 22,000 genes in the human body, understanding how spelling mistakes (variants) can cause disease or increase the risk of disease within a family can be complicated and confusing.*

*Genetic counsellors help to translate complex scientific data into more understandable, relatable and personable information regarding risk and predisposition to disease. They can also help to facilitate a discussion about genetic testing and reproductive options, often at emotional and stressful times. Genomic counselling involves the whole genome and how genomes interact to help diagnose and determine prognosis, risk and selection of treatment options. This is radically changing medicine and leading the way to personalized medicine.*

*The emotional impact for families living with life-changing and life-threatening inherited disease can be overwhelming. It's a privilege to walk alongside families as they cope with the knowledge that there's more than just the colour of their eyes being passed down through the generations of their family and deal with the decisions that they may need to make.*

Some families live with conditions such as Huntington's disease – a fatal inherited disorder resulting in the death of brain cells, for which there's no cure. The impact of the disease coursing through the generations, randomly picking its victims, can cause immense suffering. Those who have chosen genetic testing know what their fate will be if they have the gene changes that cause Huntington's. Some choose to take the test so they can decide not to have children themselves and so end the line, preventing the chance of passing it on to the next generation. Others prefer to know so they can make different lifestyle choices, such as starting their 'bucket list' early, travelling the world and not saving for a pension. And still others find that being aware would be too traumatic and so decide to live with the uncertainty of not knowing whether they'll start developing symptoms of Huntington's or not.

To make sense of the science behind inheritance is to understand what genetic factors are and what formulates a sequence of a special kind of molecule called DNA (deoxyribonucleic acid). DNA has certain base pairs equivalent to letters in the alphabet. Each of us has different combinations of pairs that form the sequence of nucleotides. The process of a gene is a sequence of DNA being turned into RNA (ribonucleic acid). It's this protein that will affect the way bodily functions can be controlled. For example, this would include biological development, such as how the brain grows in response to the environment around it.

Everyone inherits a genetic sequence that determines lots of traits. For example, if a person's temperament is genetically driven, this would govern the way the brain reacts to certain situations - a combination of what scientists call early childhood development attachment experience, and genetic and epigenetic inheritance, all of which form the personality of an individual.

Despite the traditional belief that all disease is genetic, we now know disease can be caused by other triggers, not just genetic factors. If we're created by chance interactions among events through a combination of the environment and genes, it could explain why twins can be different. It can also be why one sibling reacts one way and the other has a different emotional and biological response. What we inherit is determined by our experiences in utero, from how we were born to our mother's lifestyle, where and how our parents lived, plus what affected us during early childhood. All these influences will have a profound effect on us.

European and American studies of twins who weren't separated from their parents showed that although they shared all of their genes and grew up with the same adoring parents, they exhibited differences. This would suggest they might have been influenced by other factors in their environment, both prenatal and post-natal. Decades-long studies of identical and fraternal twins, and in some cases triplets, who had been separated at an early age and reared in what were often strikingly different environments, have documented the important interaction of nature and nurture, helping to explain the relative contributions to each child's development.

In these studies of twins,[7] when there was a high genetic factor involved in the development of mental health illnesses like depression and schizophrenia, the results suggested illnesses may not be 100 per cent determined by genes. If a person has a predisposition, other factors will contribute to the development of a disease, such as difficult emotional experiences, or infectious agents or toxins they were exposed to. With schizophrenia, a person who was genetically susceptible to this type of serious mental health disorder could have experienced trauma, a shock of some kind, a long period of stress, a crisis or a vulnerability with an impaired integration of the brain. Any and all of these situations could trigger an episode, which would begin a cycle of mental health problems.[8]

Inheritance is always about nature and nurture, which implies that even if we've inherited genetic factors or acquired certain conditions, it doesn't mean we cannot address some of these health issues and repair our inheritance.

Science is now certain that physical and mental illness can be genetically transmitted from one generation to the next. Medical research is now able to identify and minimize the effect of genetic inheritances of this kind. With the discovery of epigenetics, it can now further help us to understand what influences have come through from our family history to affect the way we think, feel and behave.

## Epigenetics

> *'There is now converging evidence supporting the idea that offspring are affected by parental trauma exposures occurring before their birth, and possibly even prior to their conception.'*
>
> Rachel Yehuda

The way we understand this process is that on top of the DNA sequences sit non-nucleic acid molecules like histones or methyl groups, which are relatively simple molecules. By sitting on the top of the DNA (hence the word 'epi', meaning 'on top of'), they create a gene change. Any gene change would lead to a new 'gene expression', which in turn would determine protein production and the way we experience different ways of being in the world.

The reason epigenetic molecules are so important is that they shape gene expression, our core genetic material. A gene is expressed when we have an experience, such as a stressor, like famine or war, at which point our own cells undergo a modification of the epigenetic regulators to allow us, for example, to process insulin in a different way based on the lack of food. Epigenetic modulation happens in order to try to adapt to the circumstances we're in.

If you're a female in the womb, when your ovaries are developing, the shape of your eggs will be based on what your mother is experiencing. If a mother is living during a famine or in a war-torn country when they are pregnant with a female foetus, the foetus' ovaries will change in response to the mother's experience. When the female foetus is born, she may or may not have her mother's epigenetic changes in her body, but when she has a baby of her own, they'll certainly inherit the epigenetic changes of the grandmothers.

Each generation will encounter a chaotic or traumatic experience, as well as a positive, affluent and creative one. It's this that the following generation will try to follow, heal or act out. From an emotional and biological perspective, the ties that bind us to our family can help or obstruct us. By reaching back into our inheritance, we can discover patterns that follow the generations. It's up to us to find strategies either to continue with those patterns or to make a break from the past and transform the legacies we've inherited.

If we lived in an ideal world, or a place of perfection, everyone would be happy. Unfortunately, people have had troubles with each other from the beginning of humanity. When a child is born, the way it's treated leaves a mark to live with, whether consciously or not. The physical body is constructed of a cellular memory that records atmospheres from the prenatal period to birth. If a child is born healthy and welcomed by the whole family – given a sort of homecoming – this joy would be like a positive injection of love received by the whole body.

Alternatively, if a child is unwanted, rejected and regarded as a hindrance when they're born, or just not liked for whatever purpose, it exposes the innocent to a threatening birth that's recorded in its cellular memory. The memories recorded by the physical body at this early age are registered and enlisted to lie dormant until they're awakened.

I (Terry) once knew a man who, in the heat of the moment as a commando during World War Two, killed a young child in cold blood to prevent his platoon from being discovered by an enemy patrol. He had to live daily with this act of murder. By the time he confessed to me, that memory had been repeated time and again, driving him to become an alcoholic. How could he tell his wife or his daughter what he'd done? The fact is distinguished by the inheritance of his act, in the seed passed on to the next generation, in that his descendants will be affected by this trauma. Science has discovered it's possible to pass those energy patterns along intergenerationally.

There have been a few instances where people have had extreme unexplainable post-traumatic stress disorder (PTSD) reactions. When they looked back two generations, they discovered their grandmother or grandfather or someone in their lineage lived during a war or the Holocaust, or that they experienced a serious trauma. It appeared everyone had kept quiet about such experiences or the family didn't even know it had happened.

One of the most interesting epigenetic discoveries is in the field of PTSD, in which they've found that somebody has acted as though they've been traumatized and yet they weren't. After medical examination, it was discovered they had the same epigenetic markers as somebody who had been severely traumatized.

Everybody who is descended from these ancestors has a piece of the action, has a fragment of their energy encoded within them. If they died from an illness or from trauma such as suicide or murder, it would affect their family, even when we look back seven generations; although in this case you'll probably only inherit a minuscule amount of their energy because you're dealing with hundreds of people at that point. However, it's the wounds within your great-grandparents, grandparents and parents that need to be addressed.

It's erroneous to think that all of our ancestors' influence is negative. This solely depends on their state of mind and their character. There are those who lived earnest lives with positive intent, who operated within a truthful modality and who are known to have supported the family inheritance and not hindered it. However, there are also those whose experiences have caused severe behavioural and mental health problems, which are still being managed by their descendants today.

## Repairing biological inheritance

To be able to heal genetic factors, we need to address physical, emotional and psychological behaviours, including social and environmental influences. It's suggested by scientists who have worked with epigenetic studies that they can reduce the stress hormone cortisol, in turn reducing inflammation, by altering epigenetic regulators. This is done primarily by using the mind to make changes to the way we think and feel.

It's believed that we can optimize our cardiovascular way of operating, improve the immune system's function, and elevate and optimize levels of enzyme that repair and maintain the ends of chromosomes - called telomeres. In turn, this contributes to our health and wellbeing, reflected in the way we care for ourselves, how we experience our relationships in our social world, and whether we're compassionate and respectful and live a purposeful life or not. All these ideals contribute to optimizing telomerase levels.

A telomere length is an important measure of ageing. They're like caps on chromosomes similar to those on a shoelace. As we get older, the telomeres become shorter and fragmented when we get stressed. The length of a person's telomeres is a good indicator of their overall health, and often, short telomeres are associated with cellular ageing and dysfunction.

As we're learning about how we can change this, it's so important to believe that even if we've inherited a lot of negative genetic factors, it doesn't mean we're helpless. Equally, we need to understand the fact that difficult early childhood experiences or those of our ancestors doesn't mean there's nothing we can do to heal or change these experiences - actually, it can mean the opposite. We can embrace the ability to make the brain more integrated and as the mind shapes how we focus our attention - where our attention goes - neural firing would flow and thus neural connection would grow. All these scientific findings are incredibly positive in the face of understanding the power of genetic inheritance.

In conclusion, if you make sense of your life, you can overcome cross-generational patterns of trauma. The neuroplasticity of the brain and the capacity for healing relationships influence our inner life and the relationship we have with other people. Through a process of integration, we retain elements of their different but also linked natures.

Helena was born in Ireland in 1958 and she came to see (Terry) when she was tackling health issues while suffering from chronic fatigue syndrome (CFS) or myalgic encephalomyelitis (ME). Helena understood her problems came from her ancestry:

### Helena's story

*I'm a 60-year-old Tipperary woman and my story is the legacy of my ancestors. I was a sensitive child, growing up in a household of silence about the things that mattered. My father married young and lost his pregnant wife within two years. He never spoke of this. The famine of the 1840s also wasn't spoken of, and the Irish civil war of the 1920s created bitter tension and so was best not discussed. I learned to keep secrets, to keep quiet and never show how I truly felt.*

*After my marriage in 1981, I worked as a teacher outside Limerick city. I was stifled by small-minded attitudes and by the unspeakable treatment of women by the Church and state in a patriarchal society. I felt the stranglehold of the Catholic Church on all aspects of life. Children born outside marriage had to be adopted and young women who kept their babies ran the risk of losing their jobs. Celibate priests were out of control. A conspiracy of silence permeated. By October 1988, I felt compelled to leave Ireland, with or without my husband. He chose to come with me, so together with our young son, we settled in London.*

*A couple more children were born in quick succession. Pursuing a career in specific learning difficulties, I became an education consultant to colleges of further education in the early 2000s. It was a busy and satisfying life. But then, in 2002, I was diagnosed with ME. I spent two subsequent years in bed, watching my life pass by, hardly able to walk, speak or think. My body shook uncontrollably, I couldn't bear anyone's energy near me and I spent day after day in my attic bedroom alone.*

*My sensitivity being heightened meant I could no longer tolerate regular daily life.*

*Only then did I decide it was important to discover our family's ancestral stories. I journeyed back to the 1800s to confront my Irish great-grandfather about his treatment of my grandmother and her disabled son, an infant who had haunted me since I was in my 40s. When in deep meditation, I discovered the child was murdered after birth, owing to his disability. He was given no recognition in this life but demanded acknowledgement from beyond the grave. My siblings also encountered this disturbed infant; we all agree on the location of his unmarked grave. We've since released him from this awful trauma and memory. And as he went into the light, there was forgiveness for what happened to both him and my grandmother. I'm happy to have helped to free him, and I feel lighter and more whole since that encounter.*

*Since doing this work, I've changed from a head-driven academic to a more humble human being. I now work with individuals and groups empowering them to overcome issues, face their fears and live life to the full.*

## Intergenerational trauma inheritance

Epigenetic research from the Dutch famine studies from 1944 to 1945 found that children born to parents and grandparents who were carrying the famine (gene) modified the way they processed food. They'd hold on to calories more, which in turn made them more likely to be obese and develop diabetes in later life. If your ancestor experienced a famine, or died in a civil war, the Second World War or the Holocaust, or faced any form of genocide or natural disaster that caused serious trauma to a community, you may have a hypervigilance for danger with intense anxiety and fear.

Sometimes the trauma is inherited early, in utero, when the mother had a previous miscarriage or a stillbirth, or whose partner or parents died. This trauma can be expressed through us and yet we may never know where it comes from because it happened so early. Equally, as with inherited trauma, we can just be born with fears and feelings that don't belong to us. Until we look back, we'll never make sense of things.

There are usually signs that indicate it may be an inherited trauma. For example, we might experience fear or anxiety, or a symptom that strikes suddenly when we reach a certain age. It's like an ancestral alarm clock that starts ringing inside us. For example, when we're 13 years old, we might suddenly feel disconnected or become supersensitive, or develop an anxiety or phobia.

Other examples could be when we feel disconnected from our spouse or partner after the birth of our children. Or we might suddenly feel trapped in a marriage, never once connecting it with our great-grandmother who was a child bride of 12 given away to some 40-year-old man. Or whose husband died in the war after the birth of their child. What we don't realize is that we're actually dealing with the effects of her trauma.

We could leave home for the first time and enter the adult world, then find we have symptoms of a mental health illness for no obvious reason, or trust issues when it comes to relationships, never making the link that this was the same age our grandmother became a widow and was suffering from a severe grief. Or that a civil war affected the livelihood of our great-grandparents, and so on.

Certain behavioural traits are passed along from generation to generation. For example, maybe your parents or grandparents lived in a place where there was a certain threat, subsequently passing on an awareness of that threat to the next generation, even transmitting it further down. This gene shifts epigenetically and could affect traits, habits, moods and intrinsic beliefs. All kinds of things are passed on epigenetically with no alteration to the genome.

Studies suggest that daughters of mothers who were depressed have the same epigenetic tags as their mothers, even though they may have had no reason to be depressed. The granddaughters of those mothers had those epigenetic signatures of depression as well, even though they also never had any reason to be depressed themselves. These are all ways in which the characteristics get passed from generation to generation. Therefore, what you're thinking, feeling and believing about the world might not even be yours at all. It might have come down from a grandparent or even a great-great-great-great-grandparent.

## Healing intergenerational trauma

When we come from a family where there was a lot of stress or criticism from a parent or a family member, we can be fearful and have exceptionally low self-esteem. We generally aren't aware of why our parents or family have become so difficult and it's only when we look back to their story that we learn the reasons why.

Often, the most difficult personalities are those who experienced and responded to tragic circumstances, abuse or trauma. These challenging events can make even the strongest person critical or defensive. Vos is from Holland, descended from parents who lived through the Second World War as children themselves. She came to see us about healing her ancestral issues from her mother's side of the family, which she believed were causing her anxiety and low self-esteem. Vos told us how her mother had been difficult and critical when she was growing up, which could have stemmed from her family history. When she looked back through her family's stories, she realized that instead of finding only broken and wounded women, she actually discovered how extraordinary they were.

Vos's story is an example of how a traumatic historical event could draw out of her female lineage women an act of such extraordinary courage and strength of character, which she and her children also inherited. Discovering their stories gave her the confidence to change her self-belief:

### Vos's story

*I descend from a lineage of strong Dutch women. When I think about my grandmothers, it's important to understand their indisputable essence – their motivation to behave ethically and morally during the Second World War. Equally, they had a fiercely protective nature with shrewd moral instincts. It was because of this solid foundation and their unshakable sense of justice that they could act with conviction to protect and look after many Jewish families who came into their care during the war.*

*My mother and her family lived in a terraced house. Their neighbours to the left were German soldiers and those to the right were Dutch prostitutes working for the German soldiers. Despite this most unconventional and dangerous situation, my grandmother was part of the Resistance movement that successfully and single-handedly managed a hidden war operation. She not only had guns hidden under the floorboards, but she also successfully concealed many Jewish children until she was able to find them a suitable, more permanent hiding place until the end of the war. And all of this under the noses of her neighbours. When the war was over, she received a tree from Israel to thank her for all she'd done.*

*My other grandmother, equally as brave, managed to look after the welfare of many Jewish families in Amsterdam. She provided them with food and goods, because the Germans prevented and restricted the Jewish people from gaining any reasonable access to healthcare or any type of much-needed provisions.*

*When I was young, I was told many stories about their brave actions and the many sacrifices they made, thereby setting a memorable example. Both grandmothers were loving, kind and compassionate women, and although they also had to deal with their own personal insecurities, it never stopped them from doing the right thing. Their love, strength and determination has had an enormous positive impact on me both as a child and an adult. I'm fortunate to have inherited their independent streak and I find I also live by the same moral convictions.*

*My friends often tell me that I approach them without judgement, and that they love me for being a loyal and compassionate friend. I really feel this innate way of being linking me directly to my grandmothers. I use the same approach with my patients and clients as a nurse and healer. Not only that, but I have also instilled this ethical behaviour in my children and I'm proud to say that they, too, continue this same legacy.*

With the intention of addressing your own inheritance, the next step would be to find out more about it. Some people want to take a DNA test, but not everyone wants to know what they may carry from their family.

If you have no information about your family heritage and you're unable to find out, you can still work on your ancestral healing by looking at what you know about yourself psychologically and emotionally, in conjunction with your medical history. If you're adopted and have information about your biological family, this will be helpful in order to discover anything you want to understand and heal about your own heritage.

It's useful to acknowledge your adoptive family heritage, as they, too, will have an influence on how you feel about yourself. The social and cultural environment, as well as their traditions and beliefs of your upbringing, will have a powerful effect on your personality and behaviour.

## Finding your DNA history

- Begin by drawing a plan of your own life experiences, from birth to current life, marking all illnesses, transitions and behaviours.
- Evaluate your family and what types of conditions can be passed down through the generations – biological, psychological, emotional and spiritual.
- Go back at least four generations if you can, to determine historical factors and ancestral stories that could be affecting you and your family.

- To help you to discover and compare attributes, it's helpful to make a chart with a list of your family members and ancestors.
- The next step is to follow your discoveries from your family tree and evaluate all illnesses, transitions and behaviours as before, filling in the spaces of your chart accordingly.
- Like a detective, when your chart is complete, you can begin to evaluate if there are any similarities that have been passed down through the generations to you.
- Write down your father's inheritance, then your mother's, your grandparents' and so on.
- Conduct further research, such as where they lived, how they died, what they did.

All this information can make a considerable difference to identifying their behaviours, talents and attitudes to food, sex, money, work, relationships and so on.

---

Ancestral issues arise in many different ways, but they can manifest in ill health as our bodies respond to the pressures of old family patterns and dysfunctions. To know our biological inheritance is essential, as this information can lead to us being multifaceted and using many different forms of healing to release our family shadows.

Chapter 4

# Ancestral Homelands and Migration

*'Some, like James Brown, tried city life and gave it up. Memory, family pulled him back, he'll tell you. Sure, he says, the South didn't give him a happy childhood. But you don't blame the land for the sins of the men who walk on it.'*

Gerri Hirshey

There's an instinctual invisible loyalty that binds us to our place of birth, the family home and the cultural community our family comes from and may have lived in for centuries. This ancestral connection to our homelands holds the history, mythology and sacred practices from our cultural heritage. As we carry in our bones the sights and sounds that our ancestors experienced, these influences are still witnessed by our family's moods, temperaments, spiritual and religious inclinations, or rebellions. They serve as a constant reminder of who we all are and where we've come from – a testament to the many generations that enrich us with the survival skills still necessary in our times.

The fact that migration has influenced humankind is unquestionable, although the reasons have been diverse. These range from social, political and historical events, such as war, to occupation of land and countries, where this causes a continual desire to disrupt communities, neighbourhoods and families. Migration from one region to another is a decision frequently based on social and environmental reasons, prevalent for a long time. For example, when nearly 12,000 years ago glaciers from the Ice Age receded to the north, the migration of peoples followed in the tracks of the melting snows, seeking greener pastures by choice at a time of necessity and survival. Even so, the roots that had been put down elsewhere by our tribal nomadic ancestors remain in our human psyche to this day.

Another example is a refugee crisis, which alerts us to the circumstances of some of our ancestral family who lived through persecution, famine and war. Many of those who survived were forced to start a new life far from their family home, changing the course of destiny of their descendants. For at least six generations, my father's family (Natalia) lived on the same land in the same community until my father left Hungary during the uprising in 1956. He fled with 200,000 refugees, who walked out of Hungary when Russia invaded. As he was the first descendant to have abandoned his roots, this left the family devastated. We hear many stories from other families who have experienced forced migration that this has led to intergenerational trauma for their descendants.

As a descendant of immigrant and refugee parents, I (Natalia) have often thought about how blessed my brother and I have been to be born at a time without war, persecution and oppression. We're lucky to have freedom of speech, a good education, healthcare and a wide range of career opportunities enabling us to choose whether we live close to our family or elsewhere. Many families aren't offered the same freedoms and some choose to remain in the same country, town or city of their family roots, remaining close to their own family for many generations. Nevertheless, home and community continue to be an essential cornerstone for all families.

## The ancestral home and belonging

On the Hebridean Isle of Lewis situated off the west coast of Scotland, we visited a dwelling called the black house - a relic from times when both people and animals abided under the same roof for generations. This life would have fulfilled the needs and ambitions of people who lived on these isles as a rural community with no motorized transport, no roads and no railways, living a sheltered clan way of life from birth to wedlock, parenthood and death.

Each person played a role in the community, invariably inherited from parents or grandparents before them. As communities became affected by greater outside influences, diffraction set in, meaning methods changed and communities dispersed into smaller groups as war, disease and famine unsettled populations who had lived side by side.

As for the ancestors, their dwelling places haven't been lost either in location or latent memories. Continuing to endure within the subconscious minds of living descendants, they're passed on from one generation to the next. With a familiar echo, they call you to come home to where you belong, to a place where your family once lived, where your birth and childhood took place. Sometimes the strong desire to migrate and move away from your family roots is unconscious or serendipitous when you find yourself going to a town, city or country that your long-lost ancestral family once came from.

Many feel they don't belong where they lived previously or where they came from. They've made the best of their lives and are happy, but something is missing, something not yet claimed or made right. This often comes up after a new birth, the death of a loved one or at times of transition. When Hattie, Terry's client, heard the calling to return to her ancient homeland, it wasn't the spoken word voiced by her Jamaican mother, who died several years earlier far from her homeland. It was the birth of her children that signalled her curiosity to seek out the unknown heritage of her family roots.

Although British-born, her family were from the West Indies. She found out that several generations earlier, her family were taken from Africa and enslaved by plantation owners. The calling to learn about her heritage came when she described it as a voice that echoed unconsciously, time and again – a deep-rooted call from her ancestors.

She ignored the calling until the birth of her children but always felt this strong desire to discover who her ancestors were. Eventually booking a flight to Ghana, Africa, in the heartlands of the African continent and the home of her ancestors, she began her journey of self-discovery.

Has this happened to you? Have you experienced a deep feeling of displacement for as long as you can remember? A sensation of itchy feet and a strong desire to get away from it all? Like nothing satisfied your instincts and ambitions, when there was no visible loyalty to make you stay? Was there a longing to return when you've moved away?

I (Terry) was born in Lowestoft in East Anglia, robust in its stature as a major fishing port in the British Isles. There was no reason for me to disown the town of my birth, but I did. I couldn't wait to get away, to explore different horizons. I found out that many of my male ancestors sought to explore greener pastures, moving from their hometown to far-off places to escape poverty, to seek better opportunities.

While growing up, I always wondered if I was like them, questioning: Where am I? Why am I here? Who are these people? It felt as if I didn't know where I belonged. Even years later, the feeling of isolation never left. Instead, it birthed a strong desire to get away from the family and community where I was brought up.

It appeared my friends didn't doubt where they belonged. Some were sentimental about their family roots, others left for university or to work in the city. Some returned and appeared to belong. I knew I didn't. I left to go to work in Devon, then followed a friend to London, where I remained for many years.

I reflected on my own family story. My parents were married just after the Second World War and remained married until their death. I was an only child and my mother was born locally to an extended family whose roots stretched back generations. My father was born in London, of Irish-English extraction, and it was only because of the war that he left London. I questioned whether or not the itchy feet that I'd inherited belonged in part to that dynasty. We then discovered my maternal great-grandmother was a Romany gypsy, which would also have influenced my desire to move away and travel.

It was 50 years before I had a DNA test that concluded I'm only 8 per cent English, but 25 per cent Scandinavian and 22 per cent from the Iberian Peninsula, with the rest from Southern Ireland. It appeared there was a genetic influence on why I always believed I was on the outside looking in, rather than like others who are happy to be on the inside of their family roots from birth to death. Yet I felt I couldn't. Whether or not there's a feeling of stolen years, we're all seeking to feel safe when we're home.

To know where you come from is very important for your identity. It's why language, food, music, dress and all these cultural influences are so important to remember. And it's why embracing all the ethnic qualities in your life is empowering. It creates security of knowing who you are and being able to pass on this cultural knowledge to your own family.

First and foremost, everyone should find out about their heritage. The current popularity of DNA testing proves people want to know where they came from. Once you find out your genetic heritage, you can visit your ancestral homelands to introduce yourself and your family to those cultural and spiritual connections. If you're unable to travel, there are other ways to visit them - you can read, watch documentaries, study about your legacy or build a shrine depicting cultural traditions from your heritage to bring that connection into your home.

Whether it's a place of baptism or marriage, or where your grandparents enjoyed their lives, to walk where they once did and to evoke childhood memories can encourage a closeness to your ancestors.

## A pilgrimage to your ancestral home

If you have family still living in your ancestral country or place, go and visit them:

- Find out about your own family stories from those who may have known them.
- Research family homes and go and visit them also.

- Go online and check out old maps from when they lived there.
- Sometimes you may even find old photographs of properties and streets of that time.

It's possible to honour our roots, even if only to recall them and see the change in our ancestors' lives over the generations. It may even be that the landscape and community have remained unchanged.

---

Jane is American and of Irish-Scottish descent, and she did just this:

**Jane's story**

*Whatever I try to do in my own life, I always make a trip either to Scotland or Ireland every year. I sort of made a vow to myself about five years ago that I was going to make that happen. That's a beautiful way to feel very close to our ancestors and to walk those ancestral lands – to stand where they stood, to look out at the sea in the same way they did. There's nothing like that as far as feeling that kind of connection. By doing so, you're drawing and reinforcing those lines, making those traditions and connections much stronger.*

*The reason I think that is because the land knows you – the land knows its children. I don't care how many generations removed you are. When you return to her, she starts talking to you. She'll say, 'Get out of the car, daughter, say hello to me.'*

*You may well have that kind of experience when you're there. You'll be travelling those roads and you'll get these kinds of premonitions like, 'I'm going to get out of the car. I've got to go and stand on that overlook.' That's the voice of the land calling to you.*

## Migration and intergenerational trauma

Have you ever thought about what lies beneath your feet? How many generations have walked these paths? How many multitudes have passed this way before? How many never made it to their destination or died en route? We're all standing as an extension of all who have gone before us. Many of our ancestors set out willingly to discover what lay beyond the horizon, while others were wrenched from their homelands because of life-threatening circumstances.

When we begin to look at what happened when our ancestors were taken from their ancestral lands, moving from one geographical place to another, in some cases, the actual migration and leaving of their homeland was a loss on every single level, as well as on an emotional, psychic and spiritual one, because the land gave them everything. For the ancients, their destiny and place in the world was directly tied to the land. Our ancestors had a deep relationship with the land, providing them with their identity, the meaning for their life, their destiny and their role within the tribe or community.

The seed of migration has existed throughout history. The movement of exploration and discovery occurred in some cases as an assumed opportunity to impose controls to jeopardize indigenous settlements. The occupation of countries either in the short or the longer term has added to a legacy of displacement. When you're wrenched away or the land is occupied, it disrupts your family's core beliefs. The language, culture and religious and sacred practices are lost from your ancestral lands. Once again, when you think about this passion, this deep bond that we all have with our cultural history, which was very alive and had deep meaning, you realize it's placed solidly in these ancestral lands.

If you observe familial patterns, you'll see them go back through the lines, to a point where that lineage broke from their ancestral land and was removed because of war, ethnic cleansing, genocide or religious persecution. How will the descendants of today's refugees feel? Will they experience the same inheritance? Or will they create their future based on the past but different from the way their parents and grandparents had? An example of healing loss and intergenerational trauma is the story of Rosemary, a full-blood descendant of Australian Aboriginal heritage, of the Kokatha People. She now works as a grief counsellor based in Australia:

### Rosemary's story

*I lived on an Aboriginal mission where, by law, Aborigines had to seek permission to leave for any reason. When*

*I was five, my parents gained an Exemption Certificate exempting them from identifying as Aboriginal. This meant they had to assimilate into white society both under the Assimilation Policy and the Aborigines Protection Act. My parents hoped it would make a better life for both themselves and their children. This was the only way they could legally live outside the mission and it required cutting ties with our Aboriginal culture. Not only that, but it also meant not speaking or listening to our traditional languages.*

*Our family moved to the town of Clare, where we were the only Aboriginal family. I grew up never hearing my parents talk in the traditional languages and, despite our grandmother being fluent in Kokatha, I never heard her speak it. Such an ongoing invasion of our culture disconnected us from both our ancestry and our ancestors.*

*The death of my mother when I was nine years old meant five of my siblings and I were put into white foster homes, where I experienced every form of abuse – we became the Stolen Generations. I married twice, once at 17 and again at 29. Both of my marriages were to white men who were drinkers. It was in 1987 that my second husband beat me so severely that the police took me to a women's shelter. I describe this as my 'rock bottom', but one day, as I was looking at my battered face in the mirror, my face was superimposed by an ancient Aboriginal grandmother's face. She told me I needed to find faith and trust in my own abilities, because I was going on a journey.*

*On leaving the shelter, I began my deeply spiritual but deeply painful healing journey of discovery. Unconsciously, I was now being spiritually guided by my ancestors. I discovered how painful it was to have been removed from my family and become part of the Stolen Generations. I then discovered I was harbouring not just my ancestors' intergenerational suppressed, unresolved grief, but it was also compounding and complicating my contemporary losses and unresolved grief. I discovered that in suppressing my emotions stemming from grief, it had to go somewhere. In my case, it became externalized, whereby my anger turned to rage and sometimes to violence. After being shown how to express grief, I became more deeply connected to my ancestry, my ancestors and my dreaming totem. Collectively, they all helped me to switch on my intuitive intelligence.*

*One day, I recall them sharing the following with me: 'You now have the ability to connect spiritually to us, using your intuitive intelligence, but you must continue your grieving processes.' They reminded me that in ancient traditional Aboriginal culture, we never had a God! For thousands of generations, all we had was our spiritual ancestors who, living in their ancient intuitive intelligence, sustained the ability to connect, too. They also knew how to cooperate with Mother Earth, their dreaming totems and neighbouring tribes, because they'd walked the earth, so they knew what it was like to be human.*

For adoptees and fostered children who were sent overseas with no history that tied them to anything, there's an argument for them to feel that they're at a loose end emotionally, potentially divorced from key information uniting them with the moment of separation from the familiar to their estrangement. This includes refugee families, who had their right to exist taken from them, complicated by lost, mismanaged or destroyed documents and records.

Whether our roots are tied to the Holocaust, slavery or pogroms, or simply an unfortunate history such as a connection to the 2.5 million people who left Ireland for greener pastures because of the potato famine in the 1840s, it's the same outcome for all. Their legacy has lost its intimacy to nation, state, city or even a native language, which soon disappears when culture, traditions and a sense of true connection are lost.

Over the last 500 years, Europeans from many nations migrated to distant lands such as the Americas, Australia, Canada, New Zealand and so on. Many families settled. However, some felt this displacement keenly. They had an inner calling from their roots – a longing to be reunited with the descendants of their ancestors' bloodline. This was felt in particular when people were stolen from their homelands only to be forced to join colonies in which their heritage was discouraged, where their sense of identity and legacy became lost in the mists of time.

In the USA, after the civil war ended in 1865, inhabitants from overseas were encouraged to go west, many moving further away from their origins. In doing so, they annihilated the indigenous peoples. To this day, ancient native burial grounds and sacred places lie beneath the earth, long forgotten, and people who once lived there remain displaced from these ancestral grounds.

Unfortunately, we human beings do horrible things such as enslave, murder and commit genocide. This has stolen the basic right for families to piece together and to state with conviction 'this is who I am' and 'this is where I come from'. This feeling of displacement is like a mystery. The idea of feeling settled never comes easy for them, just like a fugitive on the run seeking solace. The land beneath their feet insufficiently feeds their appetite to belong.

Additionally, what comes down through the DNA of each displaced person is still the living trauma of those experiences, even though it may have happened three or four generations ago. This intergenerational trauma includes apartheid, civil wars, religious wars, genocide, where millions of people were slaughtered just in the last 100 years. All these nations were dehumanized and many of these annihilations haven't been dealt with, resulting in important cultural traumas that are serious, causing epigenetic changes in families who suffered but survived these persecutions.

Obviously, for those who were wrenched from their ancestral lands in the last couple of centuries, the trauma that they experienced certainly wasn't healed in their lifetime. Contemporary situations around the world are still creating issues as a result of migration, which aren't instigated by choice but by circumstances. It's these issues that affect our ancestral inheritance.

The same situation occurred, for instance, with adopted and fostered children who were sent to Canada and Australia, as well as the forgotten children of unmarried mothers in Spain, England and Ireland who were adopted by the Catholic Church. These souls likewise seek a return so they might discover their biological family roots and heritage. The importance of knowing where we belong is a part of our innate curiosity.

## Healing intergenerational trauma by returning to your ancestral homelands

One way to heal the trauma experienced by our ancestors is by researching our family history. In doing so, we can uncover what was happening both historically and nationally in their lifetime, enabling us to form an understanding of what their life was like and what they cared about.

The more we recognize that we live under the shadow of trauma, illnesses, failures and regrets that our ancestors experienced, the more we realize their legacy. Equally, there's an enormous wealth of positive experiences, showing courage, strength, virtue and talent that we can draw on, too. Certainly, it'll influence how we undertake to live our lives in a better way. And we can call on them to stand behind us, to lend their strength and wisdom to us.

It's not just a matter of naming the dead and reminding us of who these individuals were. Sometimes it's about telling stories about them, having a meal in which we put out their favourite food and giving them a place at the table. People turn loved one's ashes into works of art or keepsakes like ornaments or jewellery. Or their clothes might be made into a teddy bear or a pillow. Or they might plant something like a tree or a shrub. Or memorials might be erected, providing the respect and dignity they deserve. There are lots of ways in which we can honour and remember our ancestors.

If your family have experienced genocide or war, it's important you return to the place of their death, which will take courage and good timing. You must only go if you feel able to manage the trip. Taking a family member or friend who you love and trust with you on this pilgrimage of remembering and honouring is helpful but not essential.

Find out names of those who died in that place. Make sure you say prayers and sing or speak words from your family's religious and cultural heritage. If necessary, conduct the stairway to heaven ritual (*see page 171*). Call on the angelic realms to rescue and heal all of those who are still trapped in this location, and to honour their memory in death. It might not always be positive, but it can be powerful, as we discover in David's story:

### David's story

*My family are Jews from Eastern Europe and my mother's side of the family descended from the Vilna Gaon, who was one of the greatest minds to have existed at the end of the seventeenth century. He was a rabbi who rewrote the* Torah *– the first of five books of the Old Testament of the Bible – and lived in Vilnius.*

*I was in Finland with a partner and we went across to Vilnius. It was an exceptional event, because when I went there, I was able to light the Shabbat (Sabbath) candles for my family, which hadn't been lit for them since they left in the early part of the twentieth century, which I guess was in my great-grandmother's time. I broke the bread and we drank wine and lit candles for the ancestors, which was a very, very emotional moment.*

*The next day, we went to see where my ancestors had lived. Again, there was an extraordinary feeling of the presence of all of the ancestors. I felt a beautiful connection. In hindsight, I think I should have left then, but instead we came across the area of the killing grounds where so many of the Jews were massacred by the Nazis. One area was where they sprayed bullets on the babies before burying them alive with their mothers. I could hear them calling through the earth and at that point, I just couldn't take any more. I excused myself from my partner and went to the gents, where I started screaming and pounding the walls. I lost it.*

*I was overcome with the grief of the ancestors, the grief of that moment. I couldn't in any way comprehend it mentally or contain it emotionally. Spiritually, I felt a complete rush of emotions coming through me from all sides like a river of grief. We left soon after and I don't think I ever want to go back to that country again.*

*That's the story of one part of my journey – one part of the ancestral branch on my mother's side, where the grief has always been woven into every smile and every story from a bittersweet angle.*

When we return to the home of our ancestors, we must love where our family is from unconditionally. This brings gentleness and compassion. We learn to tend to the land just as our ancestors did and as their descendants, living far away from the ancient ancestors' origins, we have to heal and tend our inner landscape, treating that as our homeland.

Jane, who works with ancestral land healing, said that:

*At the heart of that land, there's the ancestral soul who will never do us wrong, will never steer us wrong. If we have a question about what's right for us, what's a good path, what we need to learn about ourselves, what we need to learn about our ancestors, what we need to bring to the world, all those deep and meaningful questions can be asked of our ancestors.*

*Our soul's yearning will always let us know when we're on the right track. That's our inner compass. Without it, we're rudderless. If we hold on to that and remain loyal to that, we serve not just ourselves, but also our ancestral lineage. We bring something new to the game, in many ways erasing some of the scars of that traumatic wrenching from the ancestral land.*

One solution lies in being aware of the suffering of our ancestors, understanding their story and honouring their sacrifice, so we know who they were, why they died and how we, their descendants, can ensure they didn't die in vain.

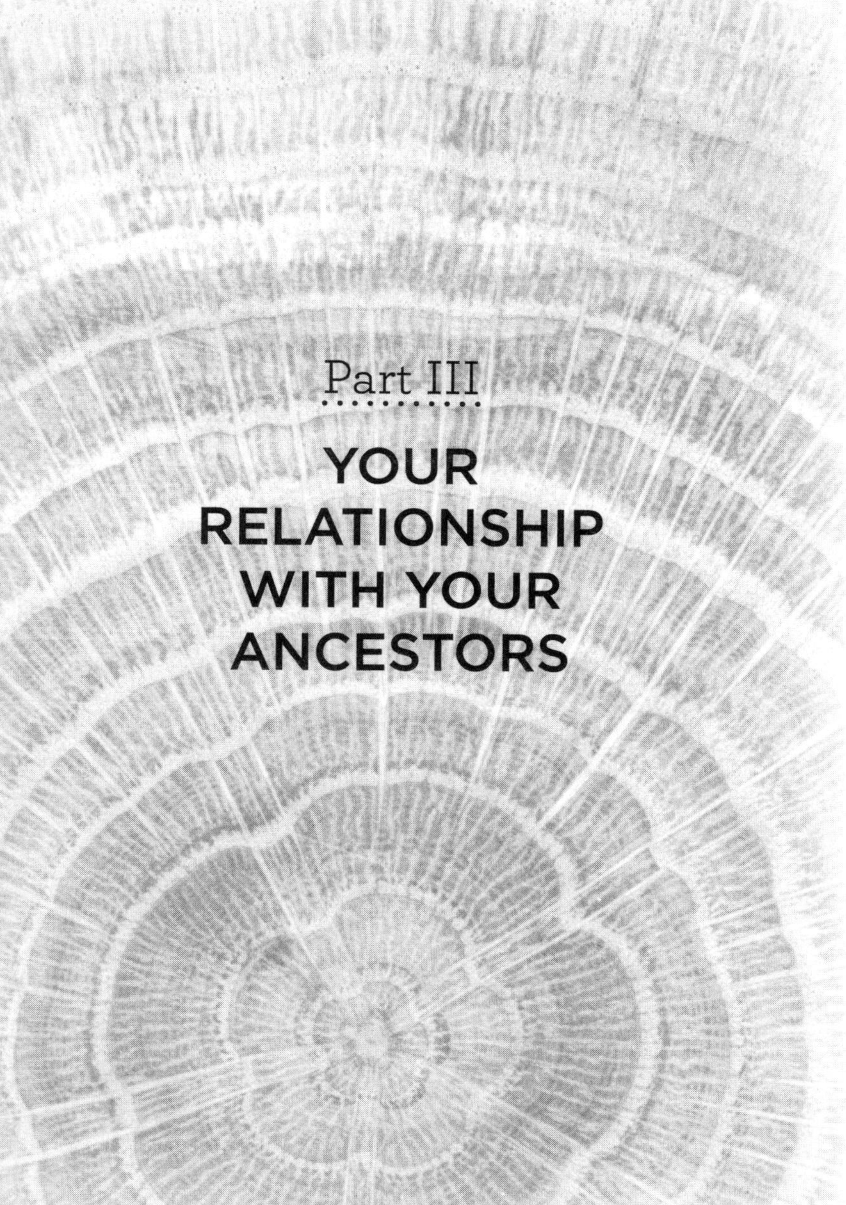

Part III

# YOUR RELATIONSHIP WITH YOUR ANCESTORS

## Chapter 5

# Healing Your Family Home

*'The ache for home lives in all of us,*
*the safe place where we can go as*
*we are and not be questioned.'*

MAYA ANGELOU

The expression 'home is where the heart is' suggests the place where we live and how we feel about our home should be both satisfying and complementary. Whether you still live in your childhood home or have moved many thousands of miles away, where you live can have a profound effect on your wellbeing. A relaxing, comfortable residence can make the difference between peace of mind or living in a constant state of anxiety and stress.

Besides, it's all the same – whether you were born in luxury or poverty, in the countryside or the city, the land beneath your feet on which the building stands will carry the echoes of history in its walls and interiors. Heirlooms and photographs inherited from our family, things we lovingly ignore, retain memories to remind us of our past, creating an impact on the 'atmosphere' in which we live.

To discover what kinds of ancestral and historical issues could affect your family home is an interesting journey. Many reflect on the places where they lived and, with hindsight, discover how much they not only loved and enjoyed, but also in some cases hated, living there. Either way, it would have had a profound effect on them. Sometimes it's a familiarity that harbours safety and if you take away that ingredient, everything can start to fall apart.

## The childhood home

From the roots of the tree of life, right from its very beginnings, branches are rediscovered just as legacy blossoms. So the land on which your family's lives are lived, the house in which you were born and raised, or in which your mother gave birth or was herself born - each has a memory within itself, experienced by those who lived there in earlier generations. Each story is connected to the next.

If you were born somewhere other than where you currently live and you feel drawn back to a family home where you once lived or when you remembered visiting your grandparents' home, there's an emotional connection that binds you to that place. Although you and your family may have moved on from there, there will be lingering memories waiting to remind you of your childhood. You may need to return to where you lived as a child and embark on a journey back to your childhood home. This experience can bring up some strong emotional memories, but it can also bring a lot of peace and healing as well.

There are many who still live around the corner from their families, just like the ancestors who also resided in that town, city or country for many generations. Some families still enjoy living close by, while others escape to the remotest places on Earth. Many of those who move away are drawn to places that belonged to their ancestors, where they feel at home. Or that dream home can turn out to be a place where they actually discover family roots.

Some people have owned a property for generations, but mostly there will be a break in this lifestyle, indicating a home of the ancestors has both stayers and leavers. A property that's been in the family for years will embrace a history that can influence the current generations more than they realize. The influences that combine in older properties are determined by the legacies left behind by former owners. Theoretically, a new-build therefore retains fewer examples of legacy or history.

The ancestors were the same as us in places where they once lived. In the passing of each generation, homes, land, estates and heirlooms were inherited. There's nowhere in the world that will have escaped historical family memories. The bloodline we share cannot be separated from the land we accommodate and have contributed towards. We cannot escape this legacy, as Sarah Jane in England discovered:

### Sarah Jane's story

*I loved my childhood home and I was there until my 20s; it was finally sold when I was 26. When we came to buy our current home, many members of my family and family friends commented on how similar it is to Woodrow, my childhood home. I couldn't see it at first, but then it became obvious, from the fact it was a blend of an old cottage (1600s) though to the 1920s to later extensions. Even the layout of the house is incredibly similar, with the kitchen at one end, the sitting room at the other and remaining rooms falling into similar positions.*

*Sometimes when I wake up, I think I'm back in Woodrow – sleeping in the bedroom that used to be at the far end of the house, just as our bedroom is now. When Terry came down to clear the house, he said he'd had dreams of a house the night before he came, but when he arrived, it wasn't the same house he'd dreamed of. Later that day, he saw a drawing of my childhood home hanging on the wall and said, 'This was the house in my dreams.' I feel I've brought with me to our new family home both Woodrow – with its homely, familiar feel – and the ancestors who related to me.*

Making connections to your family heritage is important. So many families have moved far from their ancestral home, but the connection to their heritage remains inside them. When you discover your family legacy, you can decide to return to where your family's roots are and discover the places where they once lived and died, taking this return as a pilgrimage to discover more of your family history.

## Healing your family home

The land, culture, history and family legacy all have influences on where we live today. The connections we have to any property links us to the memories from earlier times. We may well come from a town or village that consists of various family alliances, all living in different streets but commonly connected by the same bloodlines, which in some cases go back for generations. When families have moved away, it's more difficult to find this association, but whatever your circumstances, whether you can trace your family history back generations or otherwise, the question remains: How is my home being affected by my ancestors?

If you've inherited a property that's been passed down through generations, it's more likely the place feels atmospheric and gripped by its family history. The home where we live now is often filled with memories. In the passing of each generation, heirlooms are inherited by being passed down. They may hold a special meaning to the new owner, something to be treasured or honoured, but other less sentimental or valuable items may be thrown in the loft, shed or basement, left to depreciate or just be forgotten.

This often happens when we begin to fill up our homes with paraphernalia or objects considered of little material value or use but have some sentimental value attached to them.

Family heirlooms are objects that include anything from war medals and jewellery handed down from generation to generation, to exclusive antiques, a battered rocking chair, a grandmother's lock of hair, ancestral portraits, old mirrors and various other objects, all carrying both positive and negative energy from our family. They usually hold a force of their own, because the more an object is handled or treasured, the more it can manifest an emotional content that connects it to the person who treated it as special.

After the death of a relative, when their belongings are handled, it can be uncovered that there's so much more to who they were and what their life was about. We find out more about their homes, belongings, family heirlooms, jewellery, photographs and so on. All tell a story about the family heritage. Sometimes these things will bring up some particularly challenging emotions and become a doorway to the authentic character of the relative – even secrets of hidden treasures may be brought to light.

It's appropriate to take care of and respect items inherited from the deceased family member. These things once held importance to our loved one. They were openly valued by them, each item having a charge of life. Those who owned and handled these memorabilia put their essence in these collections, with some items being more intimate than others.

There's a skill called psychometry that, when applied by a skilled interpreter, can identify and translate memories of influences that have been retained in objects. When a person dies, they leave behind the whole of their life in their possessions. These are mementoes of their times, demonstrating an archaeology of sorts, of how they lived. A photograph may depict a relative in a scene frozen in time, as an image that will eventually fade. However, the feelings may not be so clear. A picture is always an echo involving past history that an ancestor can still connect through. Similarly, comparable to a series of photographs on the wall, they can represent an altar, like a doorway to the past.

When clearing an ancestral atmosphere, on some level you're identifying with aspects of someone's life that still resonate with your family. It has the power to influence you in the process of clearing out the unwanted, outdated things that hold an emotional charge. If you start to feel too attached or blocked by these objects, then it's time to consider the hold they have over you. It's worth spending time choosing what you want to keep or wish to throw away.

The benefit of letting go is that it would lift the mood. Removing old influences would free the ancestral hold, thereby creating a fresh, clean space for change. Just like our nervous system outlined like a grid, your home is set on a vibrational network that's affected day in, day out. This energy accumulates over time and becomes heavier until in most cases the atmosphere needs an outlet, affecting either electrical appliances or creating blockages in the water system, persisting until the energy gets rectified.

We all strive to have a peaceful and harmonious home. If we are content with the atmosphere, the home will be settled; otherwise it can have a fragmented atmosphere, causing distress, disharmony and imbalance. It's important to get to know your home and how the ancestral influences can affect you.

## Identifying atmospheres in your home

An atmosphere isn't always easy to interpret, understand or discern, because it can be influenced or affected either inside the building or outside by the surrounding environment. Everything has a vibrational memory, which emits a connection to the past and can have an impact on us, either negative or positive. Singularly or as a group, this energy creates the influence, either as a collection of pressures coming from the land or as the history and the property all combining to impact the atmosphere. As we're connected to everything on this planet - all animate and inanimate objects - this has a profound effect on our wellbeing.

People who have owned a property that's been in the family for generations will find themselves embracing a history that can affect current generations more than they realize. The influences that combine in older properties are determined by the legacies that have been left behind by its former owners. Instead of inheriting a property, others will choose to buy a new one or build their own home. It's necessary to become perceptive of where we live if the land has been occupied for many generations.

Similarly, a family may inherit a former slave plantation in any part of the world. Or it might be a property in London's East End that endured times of poverty, which was passed on from one generation of residents to the next, who endured a spiral of destitution living in slums built on land that had formerly been docks supporting trade and empire. Alternatively, new homes might be built on sites of former psychiatric hospitals or burial grounds, or be converted from industrial premises, public houses and old schools. There's nowhere in the world that can escape historical memories. In any event, whether you live in a new or old property, the land on which it's built will have its own atmosphere.

The history of a building holds the imprint of existence of everyone who lived and died there. The atmosphere still apportions the smells and characteristics of bygone days. You can change the decor to create a different ambience, but only the memories of the past will be covered up with a tincture of colour, not their essence.

There may be rooms in your house that you love being in more than others. If you're aware of these differences, your senses intuitively mirror a subliminal mood, compared to something you don't feel happy with. Even things we lovingly ignore retain memories to remind us of the rites of passage when it comes to birth, marriage and death. For example, a faded photograph, family heirlooms and interiors in each room resonate a mood reflecting joy, fears and worries.

When we moved to the house we bought more than 20 years ago, there was a room that, unlike other rooms in the house, was as cold as ice. To the experienced psychic, this atmosphere instinctively suggests a haunting. On this occasion, it was easy to recognize the earthbound spirit of a previous owner, who we discovered had died, aged 102, in our house some 30 years earlier. It wasn't an ancestor who was connected directly to our family but, nonetheless, a lady who required assistance to move on. Within a week after we moved in, we helped her to move on naturally. After she'd gone, the whole atmosphere changed from cold, heavy, morose and melancholic to a more settled space.

If your family is still living in the home of your ancestors and you suspect an ancestor is trying to make contact, don't ignore this strong intuitive feeling. There's a reason why you're sensing their presence. If the feeling persists, often it means the ancestors are still attached and unable to move on until the issue is addressed. If you ignore them, they'll return again and again until you acknowledge them.

If you're not in the least psychic and you haven't inherited a powerful sensitivity or empathy, the ancestor will try to disturb you in a more visceral manner. An example of this can be seen in a client of Terry's who wanted him to heal his property. He was a non-believer in life after death and when he was informed that his deceased father had been seen in the bathroom, he said, 'Nonsense. I don't believe in ghosts,' only to enter the bathroom to see a footprint indented in the shower mat – a size too big to have been his own. With nobody else in the house, this encounter with his ancestor proved too much for him to assimilate as a non-believer in survival after death.

These intrusions on the home can be confusing and even upsetting, but sometimes it's the only way an ancestor can get noticed. From their viewpoint, they're being ignored and rejected, yet behind the scenes, they work hard to try to be heard. It isn't their intention to strike fear in the hearts of those they love – it's about how hard they must knock to be heard.

You could research historical information about your home to find out what happened there in the past and how that could resonate with atmospheres you're picking up on. Here are some simple ways to research information. Once completed, you can address how to heal your family home as explored later in this chapter.

## Gaining historical information on your current property

- Research the deeds and historical information.
- Investigate any historical influences that could have affected them at that time; for example, was it in an area where there were bombings, flooding, earthquakes, fires and so on?
- Explore the building, the land and the purpose or use of the property; for example, if it was a church, school, asylum, hospital and so on.

- Study old maps, historical data, locations and names of those who lived there by using census records.

---

## Cleansing your home

The purpose of cleansing is to sense the atmosphere that needs to be uplifted or cleared.

### Space healing

- Begin by looking through all of your heirlooms and items you've inherited.
- Decide whether you want to keep them, sell them or give them away.
- If you want your descendants to inherit any of the objects, it's important you make them a box that you can pass on to them when the time is right.
- If they're already adults, maybe they can come and select items they want and then decide what to do with the rest.
- If any of the items come with a feeling of negativity or animosity from any family members, think carefully about what you want to do with them.
- Decide if you want to give them back to the family, offer them as a gift to those who wish to have them, give them away, or sell them on and use the proceeds to benefit your descendants.

These steps are all helpful to clear the ancestral atmosphere in a generous and conducive manner.

Practise these house-cleansing techniques on a regular basis to help purify and improve the atmosphere in your home and clear the space of bad energy. This is particularly helpful after ancestral healing meditations or rituals.

- Begin by conducting a space healing by lighting the end of a sage stick with a match or candle and letting it burn for a few seconds. (If you prefer, you can burn incense instead, or spray aromatherapy oils, particularly cedarwood, which is good for shifting stagnant emotional energy.)
- Blow out or extinguish the flame, leaving glowing embers smouldering.
- To infuse the space, allow the incense or sage to remain burning safely in a receptacle or bowl to catch any ashes for at least 20 minutes.
- During this time, disperse the incense or smoke from the receptacle or bowl by walking in a clockwise direction around the room, using your hand or a feather to waft the smoke into all areas, including corners and small spaces that can collect negative energy. The smoke from the incense or sage is what does the cleansing.
- Continue this process into the adjacent room and so on.
- After the cleansing is complete, open all the windows and doors to release the smoke or scent. This ensures that the negative flow of energy lifted from the atmosphere can find a route out of the house.
- You can combine burning sage with playing chimes, beating gongs, shaking rattles, ringing bells, playing singing bowls, or chanting or singing, so the sound reaches the corners of each room to lift the atmosphere.

- Sound brings to the surface the negative and positive atmospheres of each room, aggravating any unnatural or dysfunctional energy that may be just below the surface atmosphere.
- Upon completion, give thanks by using your own words or referencing a prayer for protection as closure to the proceedings.

---

## The sensitive child and the family home

The phrase 'walls have ears' is an expression meaning the older the dwelling, the greater the likelihood of it containing substantially more negative influences. Over time, these get converted into memories, becoming infused in porous materials that surround our homes. The voices of the ancestors or other earthbound spirits can still be active in these porous structures.

When a child is born to the family, the birth is generally celebrated. The family home may be decked out with signs of welcome, introducing the child to daily routines. It takes time for the sensitivity of the child and the atmosphere of its surroundings to reveal whether both coexist without complaint.

An oversensitive newborn will react to its surroundings by expressing its approval or otherwise through crying or not sleeping, or feeling agitated and uncomfortable with where they're put to sleep. The young are particularly susceptible when it comes to an ancestor's attachment, commonly from birth, then more apparently during the ages of three to four, and again during puberty – a child being the most sensitive member of the family, regardless of whether or not it's an ancestral family home or the ancestors are attached to family members. Sometimes it's to do with the atmosphere of the house, where there are ghosts or earthbound spirits. Family pets can also pick up on these atmospheres and react by displaying anxiety, particularly in certain rooms of the house.

During these ages, there's a period of cognitive development in which a child who is already predestined to being sensitive discovers how atmospheres can affect them. As a result, they complain that they're feeling uncomfortable or afraid. This is when the ancestral spirits can come and try to connect with them, which can leave the doorway between dimensions left slightly ajar, subjecting them to a variation of impulses and influences, some exceedingly kind and others not so.

It's the ancestors coming to make themselves known, especially if it's the child's guardian ancestor. Or it could be troublesome and demanding ones. Either way, they'll all need to be addressed by parents who are open-minded and mindful that their child is being affected by an ancestral presence. It's more common than most parents assume and once it's confronted by simply acknowledging that the ancestors are there and by doing some of the practices in Chapter 8 (*see pages 190–205*), they'll find that the agitation calms down.

While disturbances created by the ancestors can affect sensitive children, those children can also pick up on changes in atmosphere and emotional upheavals within the living family unit. Children often express behaviours such as fear of going to bed or going to sleep, not wanting to be left alone in the house, waking up frequently and refusing to return to sleep, or refusing to be in their bedroom on their own. This often suggests that they sense someone is in their room with them, making them feel uncomfortable or unsafe.

If you have such a child, putting them in a different bedroom or moving their bed so it faces in an alternative direction may help. But if it's the house or an ancestral interference affecting the child, these measures won't help. We recommend you believe your child if they're telling you that they're feeling frightened. Listen to them and don't automatically think they're making these feelings up.

Bedtime is a crucial time for sensitivities to expose themselves to atmospheres or the presence of spirits or ancestors. If they wake at night and they don't grow out of it, this is the child's sensitivity, which can make them feel vulnerable, as was the case with Ntesislava:

### Ntesislava's story

*Ever since I can remember, I've been sensitive to outside energies. I was always able to tell if my parents had had an argument or if there was something wrong, even though everyone in the room acted completely normal. It was a feeling, like a pressure that would increase as the atmosphere changed. I'd always assumed everyone felt it and that it was normal.*

*This sensitivity has been with me throughout my childhood and now and again I became very closed, subconsciously protecting myself. At the time I didn't know how to deal with it, as a belief in energy or spirits was always dismissed by my family as make-believe. I can see now how my oversensitivity contributed to much of my anxiety, where I felt uncomfortable in my own skin and unsure of myself. I could see how different I was to others around me, which to my misfortune led me to think there was something inherently wrong with me.*

*As I began to delve more into spirituality and the afterlife, I began to realize I'm not only affected by the living, but by the dead, too. I remember many times while I was young waking in the middle of the night to feel a presence in the room. My sister was normally sound asleep. I'd put the covers over my head and pretend I was imagining things. Sometimes it would get so terrifying I had to call my parents in the middle of the night, as I was scared this presence could harm me.*

*Looking back, I know what I was feeling was indeed a real spirit, maybe that of an ancestor. Being told this was 'only in my imagination' affected my ability to trust myself and my own feelings, as deep down we always have an instinctive knowing of what's real for us, especially as a kid. And from a young age, it's crucial to equip ourselves with knowledge of the spirit world, so we know how to deal with it instead of being afraid of it.*

## Embracing sensitivity

- Meditate alone or with other family members at your family altar and ask for ancestral guidance and protection.
- Listen to your children – be mindful of how they're feeling about their sensitivity.
- Offer your children simple relaxation techniques and mindful meditations to draw their focus away from their fears to more positive feelings.
- Ask them to write or draw what they see and feel.
- Sit by the ancestral altar for a time to pray or meditate, or just sit still and relax and be gentle with them.

In the same way that you'd respect a religious building or sanctuary, withdraw in silence and treat sensitivities with reverence. Never underestimate the powerful effects psychic sensitivity has on the mind, body and spirit.

## Chapter 6

# Earthbound Ancestors

*'It is conceivable that a spirit is Earthbound because of the life it led when in this world.'*

ELLIOT O'DONNELL

The concept of the earthbound spirit as a troubled and disturbed soul has been recognized ever since we've believed in ghosts. They remain behind after death and make their presence known long after their physical body has returned to the earth. According to an Irish myth,[9] the deceased were taken on a sea voyage to the land of the dead. The myth tells of both descents and ascents of the spirits of the departed who proceed after death to an underworld or, alternatively, to a redeeming paradise. Nothing much throughout the ages has changed – the concept of heaven remains as an illustrious realm into which the benign shall enter.

## Who can become earthbound?

There are so many ways spirits become earthbound, which essentially means they're chained to the Earth by individual circumstances of regret, unfinished business or dishonour. It can also be down to a fear of dying or due to a tragic death. For example, they may have been killed in the war, had an accident, been murdered or been buried alive in perhaps a mineshaft or beneath the waves of a perilous sea. Having described how someone who has died can be held back, why would a spirit remain earthbound, especially considering the family or loved ones who might be present at the time of death and the light that would be calling them to the realm of the ancestors?

Some who die don't always realize they're dead, returning to the places they inhabited in life and remaining there. Those lost and wandering souls are in need of assistance to move into the light. People with some experience of communicating with their deceased family can help by passing on messages. They can also call on their ancestors and loved ones to help release all attachments.

Equally, the spirit can remain earthbound if the deceased suffered regrets not amended in life. In these cases, many remain to try to pass on those messages of remorse and to ask for forgiveness. Numerous spirits will let go as soon as they feel heard, when they sense some of the problems they may have caused to living family members have been resolved. Some of our clients' ancestors come to clarify their intentions and explain their circumstances, such as why they left their tragic, violent and dark legacies when they died.

For example, when we were working in America, we helped a couple of clients whose families were tragically affected by the deaths of their grandfathers, one of whom was murdered by his partner's ex-husband. The grandfather was filled with remorse at the devastation his death left behind and how that affected his children and grandchildren, causing anxiety and fear around intimacy and a sense of vulnerability with their own partners.

Another example is of the grandson of a New York gangster who lost all the family's money. The gangster remarried but didn't have a will when he died, leaving his family and first wife destitute. The family ended up spending thousands on court cases challenging his legacy, which will go on for years and may never be resolved. These souls cannot move on until they know they're forgiven. Issues such as property, money and love affairs are the most common threads that connect individuals with their deceased and earthbound relatives.

Sometimes they're attached to either an animate or inanimate object. An inanimate piece could be anything that may have been owned or admired by the deceased, whereby they remain connected to the item and cannot physically separate themselves from it either out of desire or obsession on death. An attachment with an animate object can fall into either category, be it desire or attachment to a living person, or the loss of a loved one, indicating the deceased cannot leave behind those they love. In these cases they remain as one, still desiring a close connection to family. Equally, an obsession with thoughts of revenge can be a cause of becoming earthbound.

## The rescuing of sudden or traumatic deaths

Sudden and tragic death naturally shakes the family tree to its core, especially when family members are killed or die too young. Examples might include suicide, or when violence is involved, or an illness that is painful, aggressive and quick, or when shame or blame is attached. In such cases, a shadow is cast over living relatives and loved ones, perhaps still affecting them several generations down the family tree, just like any form of intergenerational trauma caused by war, natural disasters and pandemics.

Natural disasters such as earthquakes or tsunamis when people die unsuspectingly in their hundreds can cause a shock both to the spirit and to the place where these traumas happened. The anguish of man-made disasters such as war or genocide is compounded by the fact the bodies may never be found. For example, when soldiers and civilians have died in a war in a foreign land, many become frozen in time, never seeming to move on and simultaneously becoming trapped by how they died. They'll have no memory or awareness, and without outside help they'll remain unnoticed or stuck in a time loop, unable to get out of this timeframe.

Terry's late uncle Freddy Cooke died in Burma during the Second World War. He was blown up and killed instantly. For 60 years, he remained with his comrades who had also fallen in the place where they'd died.

> *As a child, I remember everyone talked about my Uncle Freddy and how he'd never be coming home again. He was the special one in his generation, the one who was most missed. I sensed my grandfather's presence from time to time, even though he'd been dead for many years. Occasionally, he'd communicate through Natalia, but he was never one to make a fuss, so it came as a surprise when he demanded my attention.*
>
> *On this one occasion, it surprised me that as I engaged with him, my whole body suddenly began to shake and I couldn't move. Eventually, I realized this was the earthbound spirit of my long-lost uncle. Somehow, my grandfather had been able to locate him and bring him home. Once my uncle felt the safety of being with his family, he was able to adjust and move on with my grandfather. Because the spirit world is naturally complex and difficult for us to understand, sometimes it takes years after someone's death for the reconciliation to happen.*

## Remembering and reconciliation

In all cultures, annual festivals, prayers and remembrance ceremonies are held to revere, honour and remember the dead. The purpose of these annual observances isn't just to worship the dead, but to ensure they don't remain attached to the family, the family home or their place of death. These rites of passage, honouring rituals and remembrance practices are powerful ways of facilitating these lost souls to move on to the spirit world.

For instance, in Thailand after the tsunami in 2004 that killed over 200,000 people, Buddhist monks gathered on the beach and said prayers for the dead. Many traditions conduct cleansing rituals with the belief that the spirits of the dead need the help of the living in order to be released, especially after a traumatic death. There are sites all over the world where these traumatic situations have occurred. The dead have a support network in the guise of ancient, wiser ancestors and light beings (enlightened beings or guardians), but the deceased sometimes need our help from the physical realm to conduct rituals and rescue them from places where they died tragically.

When our ancestors die under harrowing circumstances, their deaths carry a heavy energetic vibration that even non-relatives can feel. For example, these traumas might be felt when you visit sites such as the Somme in France – a First World War battlefield – or the Auschwitz concentration camp. If you're related to anyone who died in these places, the vibration affects you more, as it connects through your bloodline. Sometimes your ancestors will call on you to help release them.

The problem occurs when the person isn't honoured or grieved. The family effectively buries its grief and stops talking about the deceased, meaning the individual simply disappears or the secret is hidden from family history. Because they're never mentioned, their death is quietly forgotten.

All of our ancestors need to be honoured, especially those who died in tragic circumstances, so the trauma of their death doesn't continue to disturb the family. When we honour those who died, we restore them to the family tree, rendering that which was broken whole, bringing unseen blessings for the family.

Angela Watkins is a renowned medium who works in spiritualist churches in London. She shared her personal experiences and explained how the spirit world supports the living, helping those who are seeking forgiveness to move on after their suicide:

### Angela's story

*When the dead come to use mediums to heal a family discord or offer apologies they couldn't or wouldn't give while they were living, many of them are very sorry that they held grudges. They're glad to say they're sorry and hope to be forgiven. This can be very healing for both the living and their spirit relatives.*

*Through my work, I can offer information about which spirit ancestor who has come for their loved one is communicating through me. Confirmation is given that the ancestors know their passing was imminent and that they come to guide them safely to the light. Usually, the last spirit person to come through in a public demonstration is a suicide. My daughter sadly took her own life and she always comes at the end of each service. I can feel her come close, and she then encourages that other soul to make themselves known and to trust me to present information in a sensitive way to their family.*

*I don't usually indicate the reason for them passing, which I can often see was too upsetting and traumatic for their family to cope with. I'm given the language that's appropriate to be used in front of a congregation or audience. The communicators from the spirit world often say they found the world too upsetting and difficult to cope with, or that they'd been ill for a long time mentally, emotionally or physically. It's usually such a relief to leave their body and go home to spirit. They might even have wanted to leave their body and not start something new when everything in their life seemed too difficult.*

*After the mediumship demonstration is over, the family or friends sometimes tell me they're so relieved that the ancestors came for their loved one. Whatever difficult circumstances they were presented with, it's a comfort to know they're safe and now have a peace that they never felt when they were living.*

With the sudden death of a loved one, it's important to try to explain to them that they've died, so they can move on into the light. You can place their photograph on your altar and speak to them out loud or in your head, as they will hear you. Remember them on the anniversary of their death by celebrating their life with flowers, gifts and family gatherings. Or, if you're courageous enough, you can go to see the deceased's body and speak to them. If the body hasn't been found or you aren't allowed or able to visit the deceased, you can go to the place where your family conduct religious practices and ask the priest to lead prayers for them.

## Types of ancestral spirits that can affect us

There are many types of ancestors we've discovered from working with families on ancestral healing. They visit us in familiar patterns of behaviour, as well as inexplicable phenomena. The ancestors aren't only felt as benevolent - they can also be fierce and terrifying. This is because in death, a person can remain as they did in life, so if they were violent, ruthless, cruel, vicious or angry, they could still have these traits, haunting us if neglected and disturbing our equilibrium, imposing their fixed beliefs and fear of change. Therefore, when we can identify with who they are, we can also heal them and set them free, thereby healing the ancestral shadows that come from their lives.

The following are generalized accounts of the categories they may belong to as regards the spectrum of ancestors that exist within the spirit world:

*Biological ancestors* – this is the easiest place to start if you grew up with your biological parents. Ask questions of all living family members, then ask more intimate ones such as what their childhood was like, whom they loved as children, whom they related to, and any family stories.

*Adopted ancestors* – if you were adopted and not raised by your biological family, tracing your roots might take a slightly different tangent. Many find value in researching both their adoptive and biological ancestors, because they'll have been affected by both family lineages. If your spiritual link is stronger with your adoptive family and you feel a stronger sense of connection with them, treat them as your true ancestral lineage and consider them to be your ancestors. However, if you always felt like an outsider with your adoptive family and find that you have a stronger link with your birth parents, there can be value in finding out about your birth parents. Regardless of how much or little you learn, you can still connect with them using guided meditations and by tapping into the ancestral information that dwells inside you.

*Loving ancestors* – these are deceased loved ones from two to four generations ago. You may or may not have known them, but their life may resonate with you. Perhaps they feel the need to take care of their descendants because they died young or left their family. Or maybe there were circumstances out of their control that they feel they can amend from spirit. Their loving kindness can in some cases result in overprotection of their descendants to the detriment of their evolution.

*The protagonists of abuse and power* – this is where there are grievances or certain behaviours and shame they still hold from when they were alive. Hidden loyalties are difficult to understand, but by looking into your family history, you can find them and create a sense of liability for their actions.

*The mad and the bad ancestors* – these are the shameful, hidden and lost individuals, from the mad and sad to the evil and cruel. These characters need to be acknowledged and freed from the family story. Hidden issues create greater shadows, as what's unknown or unspoken returns as trauma in future descendants.

*The tragic ancestors* – the ones who died under distressing and traumatic circumstances through natural and man-made (war and genocide) disasters, where the body was never found, recovered or retrieved from the battlefields.

*The forgotten children* – these are the miscarriages, abortions and stillbirths. The sick or unwanted children, any abandoned or lost. These children should be remembered, acknowledged and given a rightful place in family history, as they're often hidden away.

*The collective shadow or historical ancestral legacy* – this can feel like an ancestor but it's not. Created in each generation, this is caused by circumstances and family choices such as migration, separations, financial or health traumas, and national and international events like war, natural disasters and famine.

*Publicly known ancestors* – these are iconic characters within your family. Those who were martyrs, kings, queens, political leaders, local leaders, feminists and suffragettes – the first of their generation to change the worlds of their community, nation and family. How did they change the world during their lifetime? What made them unique? What were their passions, creativity and vision?

*Spiritual ancestors* – part of your spiritual ancestry, the sense of union with your spiritual predecessors can provide even today a sense of belonging that transcends limited notions of families, clans, classes or nations of human beings who support the family with moral, ethical and intuitive wisdom.

*Ancestral archetypes* – inspirational influencers of their generation who have made a mark in history. These aren't necessarily connected to your family but leaders who have influenced our ancestors' political, religious and cultural backgrounds and are usually responsible for guiding the collective heritage of people or tribes.

## Releasing earthbound ancestors

The saying goes, 'If you love them, set them free.' This pertains to our relationship with everyone we love. All of us who have attended a funeral or cremation would have witnessed emotional turbulence among the attendees. When someone we love dies, they take with them a little part of us and we feel that loss.

We want things to return to how they were before and we can feel stuck in an emotional tug of war, where grief holds on to them. They, in turn, are seduced by the magnetism of the love, regret and loss that demands them to stay. Unbeknown to the living, a struggle ensues. Their collective energy and desire to want things to remain the same calls the spirit back from the land of the dead. For the earthbound spirit, they've lost their way, because the light they saw at their death has disappeared. They've missed that moment of letting go and moving on.

The most common reason for an earthbound ancestor being held back is when they're trying to help but instead they're becoming an obstacle. They're trying to help you with their limited skills from their time and things have moved on, so they can't. Sometimes they can be overprotective, almost helping too much. This starts having a negative effect and then it becomes an obstruction, which is when you need to release them.

## Loving attachments

As a child, Carla never met her grandparents. Her mother had always told her that her own mother was particularly loving and that she died when Carla was a child:

### Carla's story

*As a sensitive child, I knew my grandmother was with me after she passed away. My grandmother said she loved me so much. She was always trying to help me and was constantly there, but as an adult, it was getting to a point where it was suffocating. I was now a practising healer and during my training as a soul rescuer, Terry said to me: 'Wow, you're so heavy. You've got an ancestral attachment. We need to remove her.'*

*I was very confused, as I loved her. I didn't really want her to leave and I felt guilty, as if I were ungrateful for all that she'd done for me. But at the same time, I was getting so heavy physically that I could barely move. It was time to let her go. And that was what we did. I immediately felt lighter afterwards. I still call her spiritually and feel her connection, but she no longer remains attached.*

There are those deceased family members you didn't know personally, whose descendant might need love and support, but this is often to the detriment of their own necessity to move on into the light so they can be with their own ancestral family. The release of these beloved ancestors can be done around the anniversary of their death, when you feel their connection with you. Honour them at their graveside, at the family altar, in their church or place of worship. A letting-go ritual is an act of loving-kindness.

This can give a wonderful sense of relief for the living. However, some earthbound ancestors are obsessive and controlling. An obsession can indicate a grievance over a long time. There are a couple of extreme instances of a person's obsession beyond the grave in our own family. An example of a short-term obsession is Natalia's father, who was told he had just six months to live. But that wasn't the problem. The issue was that he died only two weeks after diagnosis, leaving behind much unfinished business, leading to his obsession. This was later addressed by a visit to Hungary to bury his ashes. The second example is more long-term, seen in the way Terry's mother never forgave him for leaving Lowestoft. In both cases, their obsessions temporarily led to them being left earthbound. Many who die aren't aware that they're obsessing, but with their continuing obsession, they limit their chances of moving on and those of their descendants, too.

There's a difference between an obsession and an attachment and unconditional love and support. Learning to know the difference between these personalities is based on understanding who they were in life. If they were unloving and selfish, the releasing of these souls requires forgiveness. Even if we cannot feel forgiveness in our own heart, at least try to feel compassionate rather than holding on to the pain they caused.

After the death of a loved one, we can also become obsessive towards them and letting go is part of the grieving process. One of the ways to heal is to write them a letter. Just the action of disclosing how you feel can be helpful. Also, light a candle and say a prayer at your family altar. Ask to be able to forgive and let them go. Many of the guardian ancestors are never too far away and they can be of support at this time.

## Releasing earthbound ancestors

- Set their photograph on your family altar, light a candle and sit quietly as you ask for help.
- Write them a letter and place it on the altar with their photograph, or you can simply write their name on a piece of paper:
- Say out loud or in your mind the following prayer:

  *You have travelled a long and winding road on this journey called life. None of us knows what will happen from here, but if you look deep inside, deep in your soul, you know that birth is not a beginning and death will not be the ending. Remember when you were happy and loved. Remember whom you loved and who would be looking for you in spirit.*

*It is time to let go of your anger, as well as your love. It is now time to rest, to relax and to let go. There is nothing else for you to do. If you are still frightened or angry, that is okay – it will pass as you let go. And know, in your heart, that you will leave a part of yourself behind with everything you have done, with everyone you have met, with every life you have touched – you will take a part of all of these things with you. You can go to the place where all of your loved ones are waiting for you. Now you begin to leave, I wish you love, peace and safe passage. It is now time for you to return home to the ancestral realms.*

- Assure them that they can take your love and memories with them on their journey.
- Remind them that they'll never be forgotten.
- Tell them that whatever they may feel about their life, whatever has happened, happened.
- Tell them to accept their life just as it was.

---

Tatiana had the same experience as a trainee soul rescuer:

### Tatiana's story

*In one class, we were asked to connect with and rescue the soul of an ancestor who was unable to move on in the afterlife. This was early on in my soul rescue studies, so I had little confidence that I'd be able to perform what seemed like a huge task, never mind responsibility. However, I just went with the flow, following Terry's instructions, who was guiding us on this sacred journey of connecting with one or more of our deceased family members.*

*After I allowed the noise inside my head to die down, an image suddenly appeared in my mind. It was of an old woman, who seemed lost. She was small and fragile, reminding me of an old picture of my great-grandmother from my father's Russian side. I couldn't make sense of it at the time, but I began to feel a tightening around my chest and my neck, as if there were something wrapped around them. My grandmother's relationship with her own mum wasn't good, so we didn't know much about her life or death.*

*I began to communicate with my great-grandmother, explaining my relationship to her. She was confused and didn't want to get closer, but I began to send her memories of me and my grandmother, her daughter, after which she immediately softened. At this point, Terry instructed us to try to draw them closer to us through our light. I began to, but she was unable to let go of something. She seemed worried, almost hysterical. At this point, Terry saw that she was reliving the pain and suffering she saw during the war – a wasteland of death and bodies strewn everywhere – the memory of which she was unable to let go of.*

*Terry instructed me to 'beam out' love to her from my heart chakra to allow her to come out of her state of grief and pain. As I did so, my grandmother reappeared on my right. She looked young, in her 20s, just like in their pictures together. I got very emotional, as this seemed to be the first time in ages that my grandmother had reconnected with her mother. As soon as they saw each other, my great-grandmother recognized her daughter and began to move towards her and the light. As they did so, the tightening feeling around my neck and chest began to disappear.*

*When I arrived home later that day, I told my sister what happened. I was shocked to discover that according to my aunt, my great-grandmother had hanged herself. This explained so much. Since that day, each time I look at that same picture of my grandmother and her mother, it feels different – peaceful.*

As seen from Tatiana's story, there are things you can do to help earthbound spirits.

### Rituals to help earthbound spirits

- Honour them in your actions – remember them in your thoughts.
- Hold their memory as sacred at your family altar, with photographs of them and candles and flowers.
- Pray for them.

- Speak out their names and send them love.
- Tell your children and grandchildren stories to remember them by.
- Create a memorial for those who have died tragically – frame photographs of them in honour of what they did.
- Create a memorial at their place of death.
- On the anniversary of their death, hold a family gathering each year – like an alfresco lunch where everyone can come along – to share the memories and set a place for them at the table.
- In your gatherings, invite the young and the old alike to join you.
- Encourage communication between generations, so an appreciation and legacy develops with the descendants.
- Write down your own memories in a journal and keep a copy of all obituaries passed down.
- Celebrate them at festivals of remembrance and the Day of the Dead – a Mexican celebration held annually to remember those who have died (*see page 232*).
- Remember: it takes more than one person to heal the whole of the ancestral line.

---

A ritual practice called the stairway to heaven can be used to support the release of earthbound spirits. It's a method that can be used to connect with ancestors who reside in a spiritual or intellectual light. When the ancestors arrive at the threshold of consciousness in the sheaths of dreams and imagination, wiser ancestral spirits come to assist those who need to be helped to move further into the light within the spirit world.

We can initiate healing for earthbound spirits not only through various techniques that help the process along, but also through our determination and self-awareness to heal. Change doesn't have to happen all at once but can become a part of an ongoing process for them, so they can integrate what they've learned from their experiences in life and become a part of the bigger ancestral family.

The idea behind the stairway to heaven is that ancestors arrive at the threshold of consciousness to ask questions, impart knowledge and peel away the layers of their identity. After all, by what means would we hold in balance the worlds of the natural and supernatural if not for their spiritual direction?

You can conduct this next ritual on the anniversary of their death, at places that have witnessed traumatic or sudden deaths, and in homes that appear to be haunted. Take care to familiarize yourself with the technique of linking in before you congregate together in front of the altar.

### The stairway to heaven

- Make yourself comfortable, close your eyes and take a few deep breaths. If you draw breath in through your mouth and out through your nose, it'll help you to focus. Reverse breathing helps when you need to change your mindset.

- Now you're settling down and relaxing, move your focus to the sun as an inspiration for light.
- The brightness of the sun is radiant, shining brightly just as if it were the doorway to heaven.
- Draw the image of the rays of the sun on your altar.
- From the altar, envisage light filling the room, flooding throughout your body.
- Really feel its glow and the warmth on your face.
- Feel your spirit being drawn towards the light, sensing its almighty power, just like you're being awakened.
- As the light expands your consciousness, you'll sense movement whereby a golden stairway takes form and descends from the heavens to the Earth.
- Once it settles, you may observe spirit beings acknowledging the connection you've made.
- Call the ancestors who have passed over.
- Tell the deceased that they need to look for the light and see the stairway, see who is waiting for them.
- Assure them it's okay for them to go and that they need not fear.
- Encourage them to embrace being free.

---

Once the departed ancestors have ascended the stairway to heaven, they've transcended beyond the gravitational pull of the Earth's magnetic field, disconnecting entirely from the mortal body. From this point, they've entered the kingdom of heaven to join their ancestral family and beyond. The freedom of transcending the physical body is experienced as a state of bliss without the suffering of being physical. The liberation is returning to spirit, where they came from before they were born in the cycle of life, death, life.

## Chapter 7

# Grief, Forgiveness and Letting Go

*'You should know the secret of death.
But how shall you find it unless you
seek it as the heart of life?'*

KAHLIL GIBRAN

Understanding our relationship with death gives us the opportunity to know our ancestral connections. Even if we're aware of our mortality, or have seen our loved ones die, it doesn't make the pain any easier to bear. Nor does the grief and suffering pause. Loss is going to cause pain in almost all circumstances, but if we can look beyond our grief, we can celebrate their life with vibrant appreciation.

Dealing with death requires work on many different levels, including physical, emotional and psychological. It isn't possible to do this on our own. When we learn there's a level beyond this world, it can give us faith that the spirit world supports us from the realm of the ancestors, who come to help the transition from life to death and beyond. What's conclusive in all traditions is that death and the changes it brings with it are a part of life's natural cycle. We can initiate healing through various techniques that help the process along and through our determination to heal. Healing our grief doesn't have to happen all at once but can become part of an ongoing process as we integrate what we've learned from our experiences and they become a part of who we are.

Death demands the body to be released from its form by returning it to the earth, or by transforming into ashes on the wind, or in the rivers and seas. What remains is the pure spirit of the person you once loved. They need to be welcomed home to the realm of the ancestors, just as if they'd been born again. In a way, their death becomes rebirth, as if they're a newborn claiming life.

When someone has passed, it's good practice to hold a simple ceremony for both the living family and for the deceased. This is primarily done any time from their death to their funeral and 40 days beyond to help the passing of the dead into spirit. Acknowledge their passing by lighting a candle and saying a prayer. Continue burning candles safely at your family altar for three days. Death comes with a quietness and resoluteness of peace and acceptance. There's no going back. The key to immortality lies in the belief that death is a gateway to the realms of divine consciousness.

Whether you uphold a religious or spiritual belief or not, the actions of holding your loved one's name in your heart, lighting a candle for them on your altar, honouring their memory, donating money to their favourite cause or sending them love and light in your mind will all help their spirit to find its way through the uncertainty after death when they transition away from the physical plane. Reciting prayers and creating altars, and conducting honouring practices, remembrance rituals and fire ceremonies for our deceased loved ones, all help to heal grief. Other family members can be invited to attend so you can spend time telling stories together, remembering who our loved ones were.

When someone dies in tragic circumstances, people often find it difficult to talk about them. In such cases, the grief at their loss remains an open wound and sometimes we stop thinking about them altogether, as if forgotten. But the dead want to be remembered.

The most difficult deaths to bear are those of children, creating an invisible presence. Infant death, miscarriage, abortion and stillbirth cause hidden grief around the parents and their families, touching everyone in unknown ways until it's addressed and healed. It wasn't until I (Natalia) went to Spain when researching our family history that I discovered my grandmother had given birth to a stillborn boy named Adolphino before conceiving my mother. No one ever mentioned him and although emotions were kept close to one's heart at the time, my grandmother clearly found talking about this sudden death extremely difficult. This is the case with many other parents who have experienced the loss of a baby or young child. People who haven't known the loss of a child cannot possibly fathom the depth of grief, so this pain isn't shared or spoken about. In some cases, it casts a shadow of shame and in the past, the unspoken loss was much more common than it is today.

There are many stories of children who were born after a previous in utero death and some cultures believe that the soul who came before clears the way for the next. My (Natalia) nephew, Louis, lost a daughter, Marlie, at 14 months to a sudden unexplained death in childhood (SUDC) and his partner, Joanna, discovered she was two days pregnant when Marlie died. With the loss of Marlie and the arrival of a baby boy - a new light for the family - this became not just a tragedy for the family, but also a celebration. There are so many stories of unborn children and children who died young becoming guardian angels to watch over their living family. This can help those left behind to heal in that there's an unconscious pull from the otherworld. They might also suffer from survivors' guilt, leaving an incoherent sense of incompleteness.

In many cultures, tradition dictates that the deceased soul of the child be acknowledged and honoured. It's recommended that we give thanks to them for paving the way for the birth of the new soul, so their invisible presence can become a source of love, inspiration and comfort instead of one of just grief and pain.

Honouring and remembering the passing of such a short life brings comfort to loss. In naming them, we give them existence and through this act, we make their life and death sacred. The soul who touches life even briefly brings with them many gifts and lessons. By honouring and remembering them, it makes it easier to recover from the trauma of loss. This way, they will also never feel forgotten. Louis and Joanna have created an altar in their home where they can go and talk to their daughter and remember who she was. It's also a place where their living children can come and connect with her presence. The pain may soften with time, but these beautiful souls are forever remembered.

An important way that we connect with our ancestors is in the memorials and statues that have been built around the world commemorating the dead. In Britain and across the Commonwealth, we wear poppies on 11 November, Remembrance Day, in memory of all those who have died in battle in the armed services both in and since the First World War. To commemorate those who died in the terrorist attacks of September 11, 2001, a permanent memorial has been erected at the World Trade Center site in New York City. It's designed to replicate the absence of the Twin Towers that were destroyed, consisting of two huge reflecting pools standing in the footprints of the Towers, containing the largest manmade waterfalls in North America, providing a space for reflection. And there's a Holocaust Memorial to the murdered Jewish victims of Europe in Berlin, made up of 2,711 grey concrete slabs, disturbing yet striking in what it signifies.

Collective memorials give us all a place to release some of our grief, where for a moment we can feel the presence of those who died. It's here that we can find a quiet moment to talk with them and remember them. There's a beauty in our remembrance of the dead that alleviates at least some of the pain of their loss and provides us with a powerful connection to them.

## When you must let go

The pain of losing a loved one is excruciating and that feeling of devastation is one of the hardest experiences any of us will ever have to face. But there's a process of grief that will happen naturally – time is a great healer.

### Letting go

- When a loved one dies, take this opportunity to say what you want to them or write it in a letter.
- You may find you have something you wish to do for them, such as fulfilling a dream or wish of theirs, possibly visiting a country or place, or gifting a charity or person who they loved, including placing their photograph on the altar, or visiting their graves or the place where their ashes have been buried or given to nature.
- Place flowers or gifts for them.
- Sit and spend time talking to them about your feelings.
- Tell them you loved them and that they're free to go.
- Remembering those we've loved and who have loved us in return will always be difficult, but thus they will live on in our hearts and minds.
- Bless them and ask that they find peace.

## Healing the shadow of your relationship with your deceased parents

Every time you cannot forgive someone, it keeps you connected with that person. This is accentuated following a particularly difficult relationship with your parents and this pain doesn't go away because they're no longer here. There's still a compelling need to release the past by forgiving those whose actions have hurt you. The hurt and pain that a parent can inflict on a child is often never forgotten, therefore never forgiven. If your parent/s are deceased and there was an acrimonious or wounded relationship that couldn't heal before they died, this next practice will help to release some of the pain, as much of this transference occurred when you were growing up.

Giving back what isn't ours to carry is when we leave their fate with them. When we look and feel into the depths of what their own life journey cost them – the struggles, losses, hardships, joys, loves and celebrations – in this way we step back and respectfully relinquish all of it with them. If we can honour and respect the dead by honouring their suffering, in turn we can let go of them and take our rightful place.

Even if we wish to please them, we can still continue to live a good and happy life. This way, the ancestors can see that nothing they endured was in vain. We can come to an understanding that our parents often made choices because their parents made their choices. And we can acknowledge that the circumstances of their birth, death and life in general overshadowed who they were and how they treated us.

Grief leaves you emotionally exposed. However, grief is a powerful time in which to address some of the wounds you inherited, allowing you to heal your inner child. If you were estranged from your parents or family at the time of their death, it's important you take time out to address your feelings. Be very honest and think about what happened to cause the estrangement. You could write them a letter (which you don't send but either burn, bury or keep) of how you feel about them and what they did to hurt you. End the letter by forgiving them.

Forgive them for all they've done to hurt you and your family – let them go. Liberate yourself and unburden them. Make a positive disconnection from them and reconnect with yourself so you can move to your next phase of life without them being inside the ancestral shadow. It's time to forgive ourselves and to forgive others who came before us, including adopted or unknown biological family, so that they, too, can move on to their own destiny.

## Healing your deceased mother's or father's shadow

- Imagine your mother standing in front of you, a few steps away.
- Feel her move closer and ask yourself how you feel about her.
- Do you feel open, or do you want to push her away?

- If you want to push her away, acknowledge that there are painful shadows in relation to your mother causing you to reject her.
- Continue to imagine your mother standing in front of you again and ask her how she feels about her life.
- Then take a moment to really feel in your body and heart what it must have been like for her.
- Tell her that you can feel her pain, that you understand and that you know she did the best she could at that time.
- Also, tell her you know how difficult it was for her as a child, a young woman, as a wife or as a mother.
- Start to see how their pain softens.
- The atmosphere will soften as she begins to let go – give her your blessings in releasing her.
- Repeat this exercise for your father.

This method is suitable for any deceased family member, including estranged and adoptive or foster family.

---

In many traditions, there's a belief that there's a moment in time after death when the spirit of the deceased remains close and becomes unsettled as they search for their place in the spirit realms. These are the occasions when we can address our grief about the death of a loved one and also let them go, forgiving them.

## Forgiveness prayer

- Once a candle is placed on your family altar, pray to the ancestors and spirit.
- Say out loud or in your mind '*I forgive you, I forgive you, I forgive you. I ask now that you help me to heal myself and the rest of my family.*'
- If you're unable to forgive them fully, say '*I cannot forgive you at this time, but I want you to know that this is my intention and I ask you to help me do this.*'
- Sit in quiet meditation.
- Inhale deeply through the nose then exhale through the mouth and relax as you breathe out.
- Close your eyes and think about forgiveness – what it means to you.
- Write down your thoughts and feelings, and list the changes you'd like to happen.
- Let go of the past by breathing deeply into your heart and releasing as you exhale.
- Give thanks to your ancestors.

---

We may further our own healing and break the chain of trauma by accepting their forgiveness.

Chapter 8

# Connecting and Communicating with Your Ancestors

*'I was born by myself but carry the spirit and the blood of my father, mother and my ancestors. So, I am really never alone. My identity is through that line.'*

Ziggy Marley

The idea of our loved ones being able to connect with us makes the spirit world a place full of people we once knew. It's usually only when our grandparents or parents die that it occurs to us to consider life after death, at which point we may desire to continue the connection. The longing to connect with them through dreams, thoughts, feelings and strange coincidences often makes us feel as if they're watching over us.

An encounter with the unseen is a supernatural experience. It can come in many forms, as physical reminders or unusual occurrences, such as a physical sensation on the body like a tingling, the hairs on the skin rising, the feeling of a breeze when there is none, a stroke by an invisible hand, a familiar scent that reminds you of your loved one, or when something moves of its own accord with no one present. In addition, white feathers or signs and portents reminding you of them may suddenly come to mind, even random thoughts. Perhaps you think of them for no apparent reason and suddenly feel a strong sense of affection for them, or an increase in connection seemingly happens by chance.

This synchronicity and the various ways the ancestors come to connect serve to remind us they're with us. While one person can be acutely aware of the sudden change of mood or energy, another may feel nothing. The fact that not everyone can sense or feel spirit doesn't mean they don't exist.

Your first encounter with the ancestors may cause you to be fearful because of the unknown. Or in some cases it's because of personal and family issues needing to be dealt with and you may not feel ready to confront them. Bear in mind that most people communicate with their ancestors without supernatural experiences. They come in warm, comforting ways and in the belief that they're with you. Sometimes the deceased relative might not be ready to connect with their living family. Remember: this can be distressing for them, too. It's advisable not to avoid connecting with your ancestors, as the more comfortable you become in linking with them, the more you'll get to know the wiser and more compassionate ones who are at home in the ancestral realms and come with loving support.

## Natural psychic gifts

Most sensitive people are aware of ambiances. They have highly developed empathic traits and are vulnerable to atmospheres. They see the world differently, they know what others are thinking and feeling, and they recognize negativity coming from people and places.

During my early childhood (Natalia), it wasn't uncommon for me to experience regular night terrors. I was baptized a Catholic and I wasn't supposed to believe in spirits, except for the Holy Spirit. When spirits came to me in my dreams and during the night in my room, I could sense their presence. Initially, I thought there must be something very wrong with me to be able to do this. It was only as I got older that I realized I was born a natural psychic. This gift was passed down through my heritage.

These psychic abilities were a feature in my family as far back as my great-grandmother, who had the skill to read the cards and communicate with the dead. When you have ancestors with these exceptional talents who are able to communicate with earlier generations, these gifts will inevitably be inherited by descendants.

In all traditional cultures, the ability to be the mediator and ancestral healer comes as an inherited gift. In many cases, the potential goes unrecognized, or the psychic gifted are regarded as strange or odd. There's at least one descendant born in each generation who has the sensitivity to be aware of and respond to the deeper spiritual needs of the family across generations. They're the healers of the family tree and are called on by departed ancestors who need healing to take place, not only for them, but for others within the family.

Anybody can develop psychic skills, even if they're not naturally gifted. A desire to communicate with the ancestors can be a trigger to develop these skills. It takes practice, determination and self-awareness to enable your ability to communicate with ancestors to unfold. Paths will appear, and teachers, mentors and other gifted people will come into your life to help you develop. Remember that your own healing and your individual development as the ancestral mediator are the greatest message of hope for others.

Maria is Italian, and after the death of her grandmother, she realized how psychic she was. This next story tells how her gifts as a spiritual mediator unfolded:

### Maria's story

*Born in Italy to a Catholic family, my religion left me believing that spirits, ghosts and magic weren't real but pure imagination. As a child, I remember always being oversensitive. I easily sensed how people were feeling and, being very empathic, I could feel their suffering as my own. I could hear voices close to me as well as in my mind and I always felt someone was around me, particularly at bedtime.*

*In 2016, my grandmother was dying in hospital and I spent the last 48 hours of her life with her. It was an incredible experience and ever since that time, she's come to visit me in spirit. At first, it was physical. It felt like someone or a cat was walking on my bed, but I couldn't see anything. Somehow, I started to recognize sensations like shivers in specific parts of my body and a strong vibration behind my neck.*

*When my father died a month later, my psychic senses were even more powerful. The energy at home used to become agitated and objects started to move around or even fall when no one was there. I started to receive messages from the spirit world, even though I was fundamentally in pieces because of the grief for my father and grandmother. But gradually, I started to understand what I was experiencing – and in a way, what I'd experienced my entire life. This has deepened my understanding of my psychic gifts and really helped me to value them. It allowed me not to fear my communications with the spirit world and to accept this is now a part of my life.*

Like Maria, you, too, can build on your psychic gifts as an ancestral mediator.

## Developing your psychic skills

Everyone knows of the five physical senses – sight, sound, taste, smell and touch – but then there's a sixth sense attributed to psychic skills: extra-sensory perception (ESP).

This is a simple exercise to learn about how to feel and sense atmospheres around people – known as auras. This skill can be developed to understand when you're sensing spirits around you, as well. This practice can be done on your own or with a partner.

- Make a loose fist with each of your hands, then squeeze the tips of the fingers against the palms.
- Do this several times in rapid succession until you feel intuitively that they're energized.
- You can achieve the same result by rubbing your palms together gently, in a circular motion, until you sense an energy field within them.
- If you're working with a partner, place your hands around your partner's energy field and where it begins and ends, generally about 30 centimetres (1 foot) away from the body.
- Ask them to stand in a relaxed position with their eyes closed.
- Stand 10 paces away from your partner, facing them, with your palms also facing them.
- Walk towards your partner and stop when you sense the 'edge' of their aura or energy field.
- Assuming it to be spherical in shape, move around the outside of the field using the sensitivity of your palm centres to guide you.

- Move your hands up and down over the energetic surface and sense what they feel like.
- Write down what you see and sense.
- Share your experience with your partner.
- Compare people's atmospheres by their character and their state of health and so on.

---

## Sensing your ancestors

Communicating with spirits is part of the development of psychic awareness. While some people connect with spirits easily, others need to spend time learning how not to be scared when their ancestors come to communicate. Try picturing their communication like a stream of inspiration akin to radio waves or light energy coming down into your mind and body. With practice, you'll learn how to connect with that frequency on request. Once you accept it's natural to create this connection, you'll subsequently trust that the spirit world will attend to your needs. From the moment you're willing to accept your ancestors' support, you'll see that connection everywhere in your life.

Dreams are another way they connect with you. This is when you're at your most relaxed and in an unconscious state, which makes it easier for your mind to communicate with spirit. If you recall your dreams, write them down, as this could help with the process of grief or for building your connection. Many clients have told us that when their loved ones have died, they often come in dreams to tell them that they're okay or to offer advice.

After our neighbour's wife died following 50 years of marriage, Rob dreamed that she told him to go and see the solicitor. He later admitted to us that he'd been avoiding making final arrangements for his children's legacy. Once a contact has been made with the ancestral realm, the connection will develop and strengthen over time and with commitment.

There are numerous extrasensory skills people use to connect with the spirit world, from telepathy to psychometry and mediumship. Many have intuitive abilities and can sense or feel a spirit's presence or when something isn't right. Most of these experiences aren't frightening – they can be positive and kind.

I (Terry) lost my grandfather when I was 13 years old and my grandmother died when I was 21. Having heard there were people who could speak with the spirits of the dead, I visited a spiritualist church a couple of years after she died. I didn't know what to expect, but I soon learned there are some genuine sensitives who really can transmit messages of comfort from beyond the grave.

They revealed what life is like for them since they departed from the physical dimensions and I learned that in many cases, the departed spirit was very content being in the afterlife. I discovered they were enjoying the company of old friends, as well as some distant cousins. This information really helped me to understand the usefulness of the recently deceased coming to communicate with the living.

As we've seen, the ancestors can return from the spirit world to visit us. When we look into religious studies and works such as the Egyptian or Tibetan Book of the Dead, these texts give instructions such as afterworld maps and itineraries to be learned before death, so the transition from this life to the next can be experienced with ease.

Many deceased loved ones who return and communicate with the living describe how they're met immediately after death and taken to a place of restoration, having been given time to heal and meet other deceased family members. There are protective systems in place that prevent an ancestor who isn't quite ready after their death from connecting with their descendants. In our experience, we've often found their desire and need to communicate with their descendants overrides these spiritual authorities. We suggest that if you do have a strong sense that there's an ancestor who is troubling you or your family, you seek professional help.

When you're open to spirit, if there's anything unsettled in your life, or you're overtired or unwell, the ancestors come even just to give comfort, love and peace. When I (Natalia) am feeling low or worried about my children, I feel my grandmother's hand stroking the top of my head. I know that she and other ancestors are close, reminding me not to worry.

When Natalia and I set up our first home together, my deceased maternal grandfather, Henry James Cooke, came to give us his approval. At the time this was supportive, because my mother was rather difficult at the beginning of our relationship as she didn't approve of us being together.

If you've been born to a family or culture that has strong spiritual roots, it's much easier to understand this connection and be able to form a relationship with the spirit world. From an early age, you learn to pray, communicate and know this special kinship.

We learn through knowing that death is but a transition. That to become an ancestor means to have enhanced vision and wisdom so one can be of service to the living. No matter how far away you may be from your homeland or your living family, your ancestors who guide and support you will never fail to come and offer guidance.

## Ancestral guides

> *'I have an utterly co-dependent relationship with my grandfather. When I go to sleep, I send a message to him. I tell him that I am going to do certain things and that I expect him to be there for me. From a traditional standpoint, the ancestors are family. To us, death is not*

> *an end which separates the dead from the day-to-day affairs of the living.'*
>
> MALIDOMA SOMÉ

When you were born, there would have been an unseen or unknown ancestor who came to take charge of your destiny. They've been walking with you since birth. Children are more sensitive than adults and can bridge the two realms more easily, as they still have a foot in both this world and the spirit world. Just like animals, they haven't yet been told what to see or think, which is why they're more sensitive to sensing or seeing spirits.

Catherine has been interested in angels since childhood and was a regular churchgoer when growing up in Ireland:

### Catherine's story

*I was 18 and I was working at a shoe factory, when one of the warehouse staff came up to me and said, 'Do you know that you have a guardian angel? She's over your shoulder keeping an eye on you.' I challenged him and asked what she looked like. He described my grandmother to the letter, even how she wore her hair. She'd had a stroke, so he even described her wonky smile. I love the thought that my grandmother is watching over me.*

There are gifted children waiting to be born. The ancestors prepare them for their birth and they're made aware of their destiny, so they can support them with wisdom and guidance from the ancestral realm. If a child were seeking to fulfil a business career, or likewise had musical or creative gifts, their guiding ancestor would understand that and would help them to realize their ambition. This encouragement would have been passed down from a talent source within the family tree. Earlier ancestors would have developed the initial ideas and these memories would be passed down the line to future generations for further development, finally reaching a child prepared to pursue that gift or role for the family, as in Bede's case:

**Bede's story**

*While studying for my degree, I was conscious that on my mother's side of the family, there's a great number of intellectuals and highly educated individuals. It felt natural for me to join them, so I decided to read history and politics at university. During my studies, I identified a subtle and unfamiliar influence, as if I were being helped by someone I couldn't see. I'd notice this presence particularly in an actual exam, during which I could hear this gentle voice instructing and advising me how to approach the questions. This help turned out to be excellent guidance and led to great results.*

We each have images of what our ancestors might look like or be like. These romantic notions don't really authenticate the truth about who they are, in whatever age or nation. Just because a person is old doesn't necessarily mean they're wise, as there are equally those who died young who guide and assist the living. By making the association with real people who lived and died in your family, you can more easily relate with them so that they become your ancestral guides. Some remain guides throughout your lifetime, or move on after your death or the death of your loved ones.

For the ancestors to work with us, they need to be able to communicate in some way. Sometimes we need an intermediary for this – a bridge reaching the spirit world. This is when people turn to psychics, mediums and clairvoyants, who can communicate with our beloved ancestors and deceased loved ones.

When a clairvoyant tells you about a relative who has come to give a message, they hear the deceased person talking to them telepathically. Telepathy can of course take place between the living, and some can 'see' spirits, as mentioned earlier.

## Why would you want to connect with your ancestors?

You don't need to be a medium or clairvoyant to communicate with your deceased family. Many communicate just by talking, by placing a photograph on a table or altar. Some dream of their loved ones while others experience coincidences that have the personality of the deceased written all over them.

When you're communicating with the ancestors, it's advisable to recognize what your real intentions are in connecting with them. Why do you want to communicate with the spirit world, and what will you achieve in doing so for yourself and for others?

## Discovering your aims

Reflect on the following questions to discover your aims:

- Do you want to believe that life after death exists?
- Do you want to know they're okay?
- Do you want to understand how spirit connects with the living?
- Would you like to develop your psychic talents and sensitivity to be able to communicate with them?
- Would you like to learn how to communicate with the spirit world to help others?

Before you enter the meditation ask for protection. Consider the following:

- Who can you ask for protection?
- What divine or spirit connection are you familiar with?
- Is it a guardian spirit, doorkeeper, the Great Father, the Great Mother?
- What saints or deities did your ancestors believe in?
- Which one of your ancestors would you call for help?
- How do you ask for protection?

- If you're unsure who your spirit guardian is, say *'In the name of the Great Father, the Great Mother, I ask that I will be guided in my quest for truth, personal immortality and enlightenment.'*

---

## Connecting with the ancestors

> *'What I am actually saying is that we need to be willing to let our intuition guide us, and then be willing to follow that guidance directly and fearlessly.'*
>
> Shakti Gawain

The spirit world is aware that you're in the front line of physical life and it isn't easy, with many challenges. In some cases, it can be extremely challenging. Nevertheless, the ancestors come to love and support you, to help you to fulfil your dreams and aspirations, so you can remain healthy and well, and so that you might be kind and loving to both yourself and others. When our lifestyle, habits and behaviours cause ill health, hurt others, or are extreme or immoral, it creates challenges both for our living and deceased family. However, from our experience, the ancestors are patient enough to wait until you ask for help, at which point help comes in a myriad ways.

The inherent burden of ancestral healing is another reason why they want to communicate. We can help to heal these burdens with the assistance of the more ancient ancestors by calling them collectively to enlighten those who need help. Through our communications and connections with ancestral guides and guardians, the real work of healing begins. By praying for the release of ancestral spirits from their wounds, by praying for a closure of unfinished business, by seeking and offering forgiveness, by actively addressing the problem, resolution can happen and the situation begin to be rectified.

When you unite with the ancestors, you initiate a reclamation of remaining open to spirit. In our experience, with the help of such an ancestor, you can proceed with confidence. Even your approach to life can be entered more deeply and your sense of family can be restored, regardless of how you've been parented or dislocated from your roots.

If you're an ancestral mediator, just as we did, you'll find that other people's ancestors will try to communicate with you too, as they're often frustrated with their living family. It can be exceedingly difficult for them to be heard and it's a rare gift to find a medium who can communicate with them. You must learn to ask them to leave you in peace and to come only when it's appropriate for you to help them. Naturally, some come with good intentions, but some don't and you must recognize the difference. There are various practices you can perform in order to communicate with them. A lovely, simple way to connect with your ancestors is to set aside five minutes every day for that purpose:

### Praying to the ancestors

- Light a candle on the altar, then talk to them.
- Ask them for guidance and protection.
- Say a prayer, sing a sacred song or hymn, or chant a mantra.
- Ask your ancestors for guidance for what you need currently, then give thanks.
- Choose a closing prayer, such as saying 'Amen' or 'Blessed be', or chant 'Aum' or 'Om', depending on your cultural beliefs.

This next exercise is a slightly longer practice that creates a feeling of relaxation and being open to the ancestors:

### Meditation to the ancestors

- Begin by lighting a candle on your altar.
- Say a prayer to open your connection, such as *'Please, Ancestors, come and support and guide my life.'*
- Ask for guidance, then focus on your breath and relax.
- Ask to receive light, pure compassion and love from your ancestors.
- Feel their light surrounding your body and filling your mind with peace.
- If you want, ask for creative inspiration or intuitive answers to personal issues.

Do this on a regular basis and keep a record of your experiences in your journal. While it may seem that you're not connecting, when looking back over your journal you'll become aware that the ancestors are guiding and supporting you all the time.

Building your relationship with your ancestors by dreaming requires dedication and discipline:

### Dreaming of the ancestors

- Before you go to sleep, say a prayer.
- In your own words, ask your ancestors to connect with you as you sleep.
- Keep a dream journal.
- Learn to know how you dream and whether you remember with colour, images or symbols, all representing the intensity of emotions.

---

The ancestors can appear in dreams to instruct us or foretell of danger. Many great artists and spiritual leaders were influenced by very cultivated ancestors. Great works of art and literature were inspired by ancestral spirits, including Shakespeare's *Hamlet*, Homer's *The Odyssey*, Goethe's *Faust* and Dante's *The Divine Comedy*.

## Discovering your ancestral guide

A knowledgeable ancestor is a valuable teacher when dealing with day-to-day issues, such as your personal feelings, relationships or professional decision-making. With their pragmatic approach to the mazes of life, they can help you to make decisions that support and guide your family. Some ancestral guides could be from two or three generations ago and others can be much further down the family tree. Certain ancestors have learned benevolence through challenging and difficult circumstances, while others are naturally compassionate with a loving desire to care for their family.

You can identify potential guides from your family tree, if you have one (*see Healing the family tree, page 13*). If you want to find your ancestral guide and build on your relationship, it's helpful to find their photograph and place it on the altar. To see them there every day strengthens this connection.

An ancestral guide will be recognized through their nurturing support or extended feelings of warmth, comfort and safety. As mentioned earlier (*see page 160*), if you're adopted, you can connect with either your biological or adoptive family, whoever you feel most connected to in life. Sometimes there's more than one guide, many of whom appear behind the closest guide to support and mentor the ancestral lineage. However, we suggest you learn to communicate with the one ancestor you're most drawn to. Bear in mind that sometimes it's the one who is most similar to you in personality who would also choose to work with you.

In traditional societies, the elders would choose who should be the ancestral communicator and this role would be handed down through the family lineage. It's a wise practice, as not all ancestors are suitable to be your guide, so you need to ask for the wisest and most compassionate ancestors. This is because when they haven't yet healed themselves and how they experienced their lives, they can have agendas, attachments and personal grievances, which make them unsuitable as ancestral guides. Call upon those with the highest intention for you and your family.

### Visualization meditation to discover your ancestral guide

- Place photographs of the ancestors you've chosen for this practice on your altar.
- Make the link by writing down their names if you have no photographs.
- Light your candle and call in the ancestors.
- These ancestors can be called by the spoken voice or silently in prayer simply by saying *'I call upon all of my ancestors who come with good and compassionate intentions to be permitted to join me in this meditation for guidance and protection.'*
- Focus on your breath, breathing in through the nose and out through the mouth.

- Breathe deeply until you feel your body calming and your emotions settling.
- Spray water (with essential oils) to bless your altar.
- Become still – sense (as opposed to think) the atmosphere around you.

**For the meditation**

- Sit or lie comfortably.
- Note any tension.
- Breathe deeply, in through the nose and out through the mouth, as you visualize the ancestor standing in front of you.
- Imagine you can also see the untold generations, all lined up behind your ancestral guide.
- Once you've witnessed a communication, take a breath
- Let your body and your heart relax as you tell them: *'I will remember to honour the resilience that you have left as a legacy.'*
- Write down all that you saw and felt.
- Invite your ancestral guide daily – really begin to build the connection.

---

If you consider them as an echo that influences your subconscious mind, you'll immediately connect to their frequency, just like a telephone extension that connects two receivers. A communication with guardian ancestors encourages support and will strengthen your family lineage.

Once you awaken to the knowledge that the spirit world is all around you, you'll become more sensitive to your ancestors and your immediate family. By learning how to filter the truth, you'll come to recognize what's authentic and what isn't.

Remember that you have the right to stop any communications with spirit at any time. You have the choice to set boundaries for when it's suitable for you to connect and when you don't want to. You can also call on the ancestral guides to help with protection.

Part IV

# THE SPIRITUAL LINEAGE

## Chapter 9

# The Ancient Ancestors

*'Behold the sacred hoop of your people, the grandfathers and the great-grandfathers, the younger generations and the older generations... The road of the generations you shall walk. Behold them, this is your nation, and you shall go back to them.'*

BLACK ELK OF THE OGLALA SIOUX

Western society is future-oriented and focused on achievement. We rarely look to the past and where we came from. Life isn't a long, straight road leading backwards from the here and now to a distant point on the horizon. Instead, it's a dynamic cycle of birth, death, rebirth and so on. In indigenous cultures where shamanic beliefs are still practised, death is the final rite of passage in a long series of celebrations and rituals that have marked all-important changes such as births, the coming of age, partnerships, marriages, family homes, abundance and fertility. All these key points in one's life are revered by elaborate rituals that recognize the death of the old and the birth of the new.

These traditions reach back to our most ancient ancestors, the codes and practices for which have been passed down through each generation. Each new phase should be marked by a rite of passage, as life can never be static, and change is incorporated as part of the journey. We must mark our life by holding rituals and ceremonies to honour in gratitude the lessons that come with life experiences. Reflection through prayer, rituals and honouring the ancient ancestors are all useful tools to help heal our wounds and family issues, enabling us to embrace the future with more clarity and focus. Every problem, every concern that we've experienced has been addressed before by our ancestors - our journey from spirit to human being and back to spirit is the constant cycle of all life.

Hidden grief can coil around the family, touching us in unknown ways until it's addressed and healed. Honouring ancestors is wonderfully healing - especially for those who died tragically. As a consequence, the trauma of their death doesn't continue to disturb the family any more. When we honour those who have died, we restore them to the family tree, thereby rendering whole that which was broken and bringing many unseen blessings back to the family.

Furthermore, ancient ancestors can help in situations when families separate because of social or emotional circumstances. These are important times to ask for help for affected families, particularly for their children and future descendants. The help should include addressing the dynamics of step- and half-siblings, who are often part of our contemporary society. Aim to seek resolution and guidance to enable family dynamics to remain amicable and to break down any misunderstandings or miscommunications that cause family disharmony. Bear in mind that some families stopped communicating many years ago and sometimes this can last forever, causing imbalances and leaving a toxic strain in the family heritage.

The calling of ancient ancestors can help to heal these disparities and bring a more peaceful unity for future families and their descendants. When invited to attend these events, they help to change the dynamic by bringing in light and dissipating some of the more difficult and interfering ancestors.

## Pilgrimages to ancient ancestral places

Pilgrimages to ancient and sacred places offer the opportunity to understand cultural roots, acknowledging the realm of spirit and the deep connection that we have with the Earth. Our ancient ancestors understood that the physical and spiritual worlds coexist, as beliefs throughout the world confirm.

The understanding of life as a cycle of transformation beginning at birth and proceeding through the cycles of life to death and back to rebirth reaches back to our most ancient ancestors. They understood that the seasonal cycles of the Earth, the moon and the planets were a mirror of the human cycles of existence. The mysteries of paganism and shamanic principles encourage a holistic attitude towards the soul's journey through the cycle of life and death. Many sacred places around the world are built not only to be places of worship and provide connection to spirit, but also places of death and gateways to the realm of the ancestors and the spirit world.

A pilgrimage to a sacred place is a journey of rebirth and insight that our most traumatic transitions are the ones between the known and the unknown, the familiar and the unfamiliar. This requires us to trust at a moment when we feel most vulnerable to forces beyond our control. We must gather courage and take a leap of faith. It's during these moments that the ancestors experienced periods of enlightenment. This is when we encounter our own mortality and learn most about the mysteries of the soul. For Buddhists, the contemplation of death lies at the heart of life: 'I want every human being not to be afraid of death, or of life.'[10]

The pilgrimage is essentially an external journey in search of internal revelations and consequently, an opening to view life in an entirely different way. What's required to begin this journey into the past, to seek out the ancient ancestors, is simply a willingness to research the prehistory of the landscape.

A legacy from the indigenous people of the past adorns locations from Easter Island in the South Pacific to Uluru

(Ayers Rock) in Australia and the sacred Black Hills in the American Midwest. These locations are steeped in the traditions, beliefs, customs and spiritual adherence that honour the support systems within nature as both the giver and protector of indigenous ways of life. Examples of these times vary from land to land, from the citadels - great cities extant in Central and South America - to what appear as circles of teeth extending above ground in the form of ancient standing stones in Celtic countries, such as Avebury in England and Carnac in France.

The land itself provides the link that connects to the times of the most ancient ancestors as we simply follow in the footsteps of our grandfathers and grandmothers. In turn, they endorsed the memories of their own forebears. In tracing back beyond, we see that not so long ago, a primitive formula or deliberate lifestyle connects us to the most basic concept that we still live by today - that of survival.

The times in which we live may have changed, but there's still a deep need to belong and to feel secure and nourished - to feel a sense of achievement, satisfaction and fulfilment. If we can incorporate contemporary lifestyles into the ways of the ancient ancestors, this disconnection from the natural world in which everything played a part will be connected once again with the visible and invisible world (physical and spiritual world) as one.

## Role of shamans in ancestral healing

This sense of interconnectedness provided its own welfare state in which survival in the physical dimension was intrinsically supported by those in the invisible world. This inseparable union with the ancestors was provided by the shaman or medicine man, who could be titled priest, doctor or oracle.

The shaman balanced the gateway that united the visible and the invisible as a walker between the realm of dreams and the social system of their native lineage. As a priest, they officiated in life and laid out the dead. As doctor or medicine man, they healed wounds and sickness. And as the oracle, they predicted events to benefit the tribe. They officiated at all gatherings, rituals and ceremonies concerning the rites of passage between birth and death. Examples of ancient ancestral traditions remain in the land as relics of their time and as such, they were used as a gateway from the realm of dreams in their memories. The echo of their chants, celebrations and offerings is etched in the stones, in the landscape - these memories held in the soil.

In all places of spiritual honouring, each time a prayer is uttered, a ritual ascribed or a ceremony conducted, a force field is generated. The repetition of these practices combines to capture these recitals - in a time lock, if you like - awaiting future generations to tap into awakening in themselves. In ancient memory, there's an internal revelation that they're reconnected with the times that their ancestors passed this way before.

This moment, this déjà vu, this epiphany is known as the awakening, in which you reunite with the cycle of life, a circle of existence. The pilgrim or initiate realizes their connection to the ancient ancestors, the awakening is realized and the next step is to act as the ancestral family mediator.

## The ancestral mediator

> *'My grandfather taught me that a healer without compassion for all life in his heart is like a drum without its skin, like a river without water, like a human being without reproductive organs.'*
>
> Vusamazulu Credo Mutwa

Once you've discovered that you've inherited the gift to connect with the ancient ancestors, you can practise how to become adept at communicating with them. This means learning how to pray, listen and dream, and to conduct rituals to honour and remember them.

Vusamazulu Credo Mutwa was a famous South African sangoma who kept these sacred practices alive in his Zulu homeland in South Africa. A sangoma is a mediator between the natural world and the supernatural dimensions. Sangoma and shamanic traditions of communication with the dead are similar in that they stand at the doorway between that which can been seen with the naked eye and that which is there to be seen in the rich tapestry that makes up the mythologies of the Earth. They're the doorkeepers of wisdom from the ancient ancestors for their living descendants who require guidance and support, and they carry out rituals and ceremonies for the community.

Most of the ancient ancestral communications are performed by a chosen mediator, normally a skilled shaman or ancestral healer. They have a natural ability to mediate between the spirit world and the human world, and dimensions in the kingdoms of nature, having developed skills to tap into the past, present and future. In shamanic traditions, it's believed that the ancient ones are already calling you and that they wish to support your spiritual growth. The simplest way to begin is to agree that you can and are willing to do this work.

Not so long ago, our ancestors knew every blade of grass, every river, mountain and ridge. They knew the tree, animal, bird and insect species that lived among their homelands. This is how the communities learned to connect with the spirits of place and to maintain a link with the ancient ones. Although we've lost this knowledge and connection to the natural world, we're still aware that nature is alive. We possess both a feeling and a consciousness that there's more to life than just being human. Reconnecting our relationship with the natural world would support the future of the Earth for our descendants.

In many indigenous cultures, there's a belief that everything, both good and bad, originates from the otherworld, the world of spirit. Great importance is put on connecting with their ancestors and the spirits from the natural world, as these are interconnected. As all traditional healers seek out ancestral allies and guides, you, too, could seek the wise ancestors who are closest to the heart of the ancient cosmic web. In shamanic traditions, they believe that no spirit is absent from the eternal - some are just closer to the Earth than others.

As you become the ancestral healer and mediator for your family, you begin to realize that you're an ancestor of the children yet unborn - a living link between what we regard as the past and the future. We need to honour these transitions with the support of our ancestors, especially if we've lost connection with our own ancestral lineage. By connecting and communicating with our ancestors, we can receive their guidance to support us through these challenging times, or anytime that we feel we need their help. Before we initiate a connection, there are a few things we need to know:

## Psychic protection and self-awareness

- Once you've opened the gateway to the otherworld, you're accountable for this connection to be maintained or to fade away.

- The experience is an awakening of your natural senses (sensors) and with practice, the phenomena will usually increase over time.
- Each time you have an encounter with the otherworld may be different.
- It's a good idea to prepare yourself through meditation and prayer.
- There can be unforeseen hidden dangers when dealing with the spirit world if you're unaware of what you're doing or delving into. Therefore, it's essential before you enter meditation that you ask for protection. Say *'Please could my ancestral guardian guide and protect me as I conduct these meditation rituals.'*
- If you're unsure who your spirit guardian is, say the following: *'In the name of the Great Father, the Great Mother, I ask that I will be guided in my quest for truth, for both personal immortality and enlightenment.'*
- We discourage anyone from communicating with the otherworld if they're oversensitive, troubled or of unsound mind, a drug user, or after they've consumed alcohol.

The ancestral guardian is the doorkeeper to ancient wisdom and the filter between dimensions. These souls reach further back into our ancestral lineage and they've been in spirit longer, meaning they can offer greater wisdom. The ancient ancestor is termed as a wisdom keeper of records, or a doorkeeper, with duties similar to those of our great ancestor or guardian angel.

If you wish to connect with your ancient ancestor, we recommend the following meditation:

## Meditation to connect with your ancient guardian ancestor

- Find a quiet space where you can be alone.
- Sit or lie comfortably with your back straight or on the ground.
- Breathe slowly and deeply into your solar plexus.
- Follow your breath.
- Hold then exhale and release any tension.
- Repeat seven times.
- Call on your ancestral family guardian spirit to connect their light to you.
- Visualize this light becoming powerful, more real with each breath.
- Let it brighten your aura, making its way throughout your body until you visualize yourself standing under a shower of light as clear as pure water, coming down through the top of your head, cleansing your body.
- When you feel the connection with the ancestral light, call them with a simple prayer of your request.

- Say *'I ask my true ancestral guiding spirit to come forwards now and show me their power and protection to guide me at this time.'*
- Visualize a place or landscape that connects you to them and their original ancient ancestral home to reinforce and ground your connection with them.
- Ask them to open your heart and mind to new perspectives.
- Then ask your ancestor for insights to a problem that currently preoccupies your mind.
- Make sure you breathe deeply, in through the nose and out through the mouth, and allow your mind to flow.
- When you're ready to disconnect, take three deep breaths then open your eyes.
- To close the meditation, take a deep breath in through the nose and out through the mouth.
- Thank your ancestor for coming to connect with you.
- Repeat as necessary.

---

With repeated practice, you'll sense a presence. By conducting regular rituals and meditations at your ancestral shrine, you'll naturally maintain your connection with the ancient ancestors.

## Chapter 10

# Honouring and Remembering the Ancestors

*'In ancestral kinship, it is believed that the special and timeless knowledge of the old ones of the community lives on in their bones after death.'*

Clarissa Pinkola Estes

Honouring the ancestors is a worldwide tradition and each culture, religion or spiritual belief conducts funeral rites, worshipping of the dead and deliverance of the soul in their own way. Whether you hold a belief in resurrection or reincarnation, the departed still require the living to keep their memories alive, for the dead aren't dead but merely in transition, awaiting the next episode of an exciting journey into the greatest mystery of all.

The values of the departed invariably haven't changed, since they left behind memories of their times only to move on into the spiritual dimension. When you're building an altar or shrine dedicated to their needs, it should be done with them in mind. For example, each generation takes up life's challenges with a contemporary outlook and will probably do some things differently. Remember that the altar or shrine you construct is designed with traditional ways in mind, but you also need to put aside a section for modern living, to be shared equally with love and not by generational comparisons. This will serve to make everyone equally important (*see altar section, page 30*).

## Celebrating the ancestors

Whether you're inclined to celebrate the mystery of the otherworld in traditional or Christian beliefs in the unity of souls, or Halloween (originally Hallow e'en) as a cavalcade of ghosts, remember that recognition of this festival invites us to make death less terrifying, during which sacrifices are made to the gods. Even knowing long winter nights lie ahead as darkness drops her blanket over a frozen landscape, we may prepare a table for our departed loved ones and remember them with gratitude and reverence.

Each year, we (Terry and Natalia) convene ancestral healing retreats, inviting clients to reconnect with the memories of loved ones past, honour their long-departed ancestors and explore issues that may have haunted them from their ancestral heritage. It's at these retreats that they can also learn to devise an investigation into family stories to begin to understand the following question: Where did my ancestors' story end and where did mine begin?

These retreats are effective in raising unanswered questions and helping to release issues arising from unfinished business. There may be traumatic memories that lie embedded in their descendant, or there may be an issue that causes a family trauma that repeats. Gathering together stimulates these ancestral shadows to be laid to rest.

However, not all inherited issues are easily resolved. For example, there are those who find it difficult to reconcile with those who have wounded or hurt them. To stop the pain, an acknowledgement of these differences is at least the beginning of letting go. Of course, it's easier for those who harbour no ill will to let go. It's the spoken word of forgiveness that will break the spell of misunderstandings or disagreements (*see page 184*).

In honouring our ancestors, we create a relationship - a constant connection that evolves and continues to improve by encouraging forgiveness and compassion, thereby creating new insights to develop wisdom.

## Conducting an ancestral healing ceremony

When you host an ancestral healing ceremony, you adopt the mantle of organizer, mediator and healer to explore your own potential as a lynchpin between the realm of the living and the dimensions of the dead. It's through spiritual mediation of all the ancestors that we hold in balance the worlds of the natural and the supernatural.

You can develop, explore and change the ceremony each year, adding to it by interchanging suggestions and remaining open to transformation. Each year brings a new story to the family: a birth, death, partnership, marriage, new career and so on. Therefore, each annual ceremony will have both new and familiar family members.

Family gatherings can fall into the category of warm and tender, but they can also be challenging and fraught with tension. To alleviate potential premeditated discord, it's helpful that you express the idea that there are no expectations – that you're only focusing on celebrating and honouring family history. The first time you conduct the gathering as a mediator is the most challenging.

As you share your feelings and understanding with each other, it's important to accept and support each person's spiritual path. Everyone needs to feel included and respected for who they are. The ceremony is only to celebrate and honour the ancestors, with no hidden agenda.

However, when you've conducted the ceremony once, you'll probably be drawn to host a reunion each year to enable the whole family to remember who they've loved and lost, and to celebrate the gift of a newborn and encourage those who aren't yet born. The legacy of being an ancestral mediator is to teach others within the family how to hold these ceremonies and to honour the ancestors. The idea is to make it a part of family cultural and spiritual experiences, and to include family celebrations such as Christmas, Easter, Thanksgiving, Shabbat and Diwali.

The recommended time to conduct ceremonies for the dead is at dusk. Traditionally, this is an evening celebration with an optional bonfire lit outside. This gathering of family, extended family and close friends is designed to honour the passing of loved ones and celebrate renewal, thereby representing those yet unborn. The host may ask the gathering to bring food and drink to share. If you've prepared a bonfire, ask everyone to contribute wood, as well as flowers, candles and photographs of their deceased loved ones. You can construct a shrine or an altar in advance of the ceremony and it can be reused for any sacred purposes or at times when you wish to honour and connect with the ancestors.

Widely celebrated throughout the British Isles and Ireland, the Samhain festival is held from the eve of 31 October to 1 November (in the southern hemisphere it's from 30 April to 1 May), marking the end of the harvest season and the beginning of winter and a new year (*see also page 231*).

## Conducting a Samhain festival

- At a chosen time, the host offers up a prayer to the ancestors on behalf of the gathering.
- When this is done, you may light candles that are already set on the shrine or altar space.

- Each person may then add their photographs, flowers, a bowl of sand in which to place small candles and personal items from the ancestral family.
- Once you've set the ceremonial space, as the host you may wish to ask everyone to gather for a quiet moment or a two-minute silence in remembrance.
- You could even instruct a guided meditation.
- This is also the chance for people to say a few words either out loud or in silence.
- The best way to endorse the prayers is to ask all those who want to say a few words to form a circle.
- Then clockwise, one at a time, instruct them to approach the shrine and speak to the ancestors before returning to the circle.
- The circle remains in place until the last speaker has returned to their space to complete it.
- Only then does the host disperse the speakers.
- Some people like to place a basket of sticks near the bonfire so everyone can take a stick in turn and place it on the fire as they say a prayer to honour their deceased loved ones and the ancestors.
- The stick is designed to focus on what they wish to let go of from the old year, so everyone is free to make a new start and say *'I let go.'*
- When the prayers have been said, it's time to light the bonfire to celebrate light, new beginnings, rebirth, fresh opportunities and friendships.
- As the fire burns, a circle of light forms in the darkness of night.

- Now is the time to share the food and drink, and to gather together to tell your stories of those who have departed from this world into the commonwealth of spirits.
- The host is responsible for setting a deadline on the evening's closure by thanking the ancestors for their presence.

---

## Festivals to honour and celebrate the dead

Many customs are rooted in local culture and passed down through the generations. This will affect how people practise religious and spiritual ceremonies, including songs, dances and celebrations.

There are many traditional cultures that celebrate the ancestors, enjoying an opportunity to bridge, albeit temporarily, the divide that separates generations, reaching back in time beyond written language and historical memory. Visiting the graves of our family and loved ones is important as we must remember them even though they've gone, for they shouldn't be forgotten.

It's custom within many indigenous cultures to communicate with the ancestors and this belief has enabled an unbreakable connection to continue from one generation to the next. In some cases, the communication is conducted as a celebration uniting the living and the dead in ritual or in festivals with the wearing of masks or the painting of the body. Araly does just that every year by attending the Festival of Sumpango in Guatemala:

### Araly's story

*The date 1 November is a mystical cultural celebration passed down from generation to generation. Despite the diversity within the country, many celebrate this day with their family. The Festival of Sumpango or Giant Kite Festival is carried out in the village of Sumpango in Guatemala. On All Souls' Day, people congregate on the football field in order to appreciate the kites, which are like works of art, full of colour and ingenuity, as they rise and embellish the sky with culture and creativity. In various sizes, some measuring as much as 20 metres (65 feet), the kites are often created months in advance by the local residents.*

*They represent different themes such as culture, traditions, unity and faith, as well as caring for nature, and love of the Earth and towards man. According to the beliefs of settlers in ancient times, their purpose was to rise and pay homage to good spirits and to bully evil spirits. I personally enjoy observing from the road, because the landscapes are beautiful. On this day, people enjoy delicious 'cold meats', which is a traditional food of the country, full of different vegetables and sausages mixed with a pickled salad representing the multiculturalism of the country.*

The dead are remembered across the globe in numerous ways, depending on one's culture, traditions, beliefs and religion, in the form of ceremonies, offerings and rituals, each important and significant in its own right, ensuring an emotional connection is retained even after their death. Ancient customs are observed and it's a time for families to unite in diverse ways.

For example, between May and July, the Boon Para Wate festival or Day of the Dead is held in Thailand over a period of three days. Music and festivities signify the first day, followed by torches representing the end of the procession on the second, which are later extinguished, concluding on the third day, which is marked by the reciting of prayers by monks representing the rebirth of the Buddha.

Celebrated in spring, the Chinese equivalent, held on 4, 5 or 6 April, is called the Qingming or Tomb-Sweeping Day, during which graves are cleaned, cold food is served and fires remain unlit, representing the festival of light and rebirth. A simple affair, when kites are flown like the Guatemalans' in Araly's story, dumplings consumed and goods offered that are deemed of value in the otherworld, such as tea and incense.

In mid-August, the Japanese release lanterns and light bonfires to commemorate the Day of the Dead on the Obon Lantern Day, the intention being that they guide the spirits to the light. Dancing (like the *Bon Odori*) is also a feature, as is visiting graveyards.

Another sombre occasion held in China is the annual Hungry Ghost Festival on the last day of August, when the line between life and death is seen to be most indistinct. During this ceremony, the spirits are entertained with music, and creative paper offerings like a form of origami are burned, designed to signify items or effects that living relatives wish to send to their late loved ones in the afterlife. Paper lanterns are also released with the aim of guiding restless spirits home. But the German version, called Totensonntag, which is also solemn in that it's more a day of remembrance, is conducted in silence, with dancing and music prohibited.

The Hindu equivalent in India sees a festival called Mahalaya Amãvasyã during the new moon in September. As the goddess of protection, strength, motherhood, destruction and wars, Durga is revered during ceremonies in which spirits are evoked and the departed banished during various rituals. Another Hindu festival is Pitru Paksha, during which participants refrain from undertaking new projects, removing hair or eating garlic, lasting 16 days.

At the end of the Buddhist Lent, Vassa, a fifteen-day festival is held in Cambodia called Pchum Ben or Ancestors' Day in September or October according to the Khmer calendar. Food is left out as a tribute to calm dead souls so that they might wander among the living at the opening of the gates of hell, unite with those they hold dear and make amends for past wrongs.

Held over three days in September/October, the Chuseok Festival in North and South Korea is designed to pay heed to the ancestors during the full moon of the eighth month of the lunar calendar, which incorporates dancing, the cleaning of graves and offerings of food. Literally meaning 'autumn evening', various rites are adopted to honour a good harvest, in which rice cakes called *songpyeon* are offered, as it's believed the deceased play a part in this.

In Europe, Samhain is held from the eve of 31 October to 1 November (in the southern hemisphere it's celebrated from 30 April to 1 May), marking the end of the harvest season, the beginning of a cold winter and the birth of a new year. It's a pagan festival with Celtic and Roman roots, modified by Christianity to celebrate the festivals of All Saints (or All-Hallows) and All Souls as a tribute to the dead. Held on 2 November, on All Souls' Day the dead are revered by the living, upholding the coming together of souls from one dimension to the other. It was introduced by the Abbot of Cluny in AD998, so the dead were remembered in the liturgies of the Church.

On All Souls' Eve, families sat up all night and little cakes known as soul cakes were consumed. The custom involved children going from door to door 'souling' for cakes or money. As the clock struck midnight, there was silence, for at this hour the souls of the dead revisited their earthly homes. The belief was that this was when the returning souls came back to Earth to cause mayhem and wreak havoc, warded off by spiritual bonfires and masks, so the living might meld with and expel evil spirits. The ancestors returned from the afterlife to set the land back to zero or reboot it, if you like, prior to the onset of winter, so that families might be protected. Later known as the Night of the Dead, it was understood they were able to do so because the periphery between the lands of the living and the dead became indistinct the night before the new year. Today, Halloween has evolved from a time of fantastic lanterns carved out of mangolds, later to be replaced by the humble pumpkin. Families celebrate by wearing costumes and trick-or-treating, with various props such as pumpkins, cobwebs and bats, becoming the Halloween we know and love today. In fact, costumes are now a fundamental part of celebrations in America courtesy of the Irish, thought to ward off spirits.[11]

Mexico celebrates El Día de los Muertos (the Day of the Dead) at the start of November. This holiday of pre-Hispanic origin is held in tribute to the deceased. Altars and offerings feature heavily, as does food such as *pan de muertos* (bread of the dead) and *calaveras dulces* (sweet skulls). Our connections with Mexico also ensure the festival is held over here in various cities in the UK.

Brazilians hold a similar festival on the same day during which families come together and visit their loved ones' graves on the Día dos Finados or the Day of the Finished. Like other festivals, offerings of flowers and candles mark the occasion. Gravestones also feature in the Russian Orthodox Church's Radonitsa, during which Easter eggs are left on the headstones before dining alongside the graves. Eggs also feature on Thursday of the Dead or Thursday of the Secrets, shared by Muslims and Christians in the eastern Mediterranean around Easter, during which food is distributed to the poor and children receive painted eggs.

In November in Bolivia on the Day of the Dead, the Aymaras descend on cemeteries with the skulls of the dearly departed for what is known as the Fiesta de las Ñatitas. It's believed that the skulls have looked out for living relatives from the land of the dead, and these skulls are often trimmed with flowers or encased in boxes. Bones of loved ones also feature in Indonesia, where they are exhumed and purified over a protracted period of time in order to free their spirit, and also in Madagascar.

The Nepalese use cows to usher the deceased into the afterlife. And with other celebrations, empty seats might be left at the table for spirits to occupy. Lanterns might be released and rice thrown. And the colour red might be avoided to prevent spiritual possession. Or they might be pure in thought, people perhaps gathering to pray. Another way to honour those no longer on this mortal coil might involve abstinence or a pilgrimage. These may be joyous, sacred or foreboding affairs with many similarities as different customs are observed.

These rituals and ceremonies call together the shades or spirits and spectres in people's lives, enabling us to remember that our ancestors are our most intimate connection with the spirit world. The ancestors stand at the gateway of birth and death. Ceremonies and celebrations are applied to help people in the transition from surviving to thriving, as well as to honour and remember those who came before us, on anniversaries and ceremonial occasions, or when the family need support at births, deaths or transitional times.

# Chapter 11
## The Legacy

*'It is our birthright to fully express our souls. Life without meaning equals despair. It is time for all to collect back our lost pieces and remember why we were born into this world.'*

SANDRA INGERMAN

Your birth story is the latest evolution of your family line. Each generation born in your lifetime will come into the world carrying unique gifts needed by the family community. Yet, through the process of being born and the trials of growing up, you often forget what it is that you've come here to do. The ancestors will keep reminding you and by discovering the stories of our ancestors, we can consider the story we'll leave behind for our own descendants. Part of our legacy is based on what can be done to repair past issues and put them behind us.

The legacy is defined as a compendium of ideas – lifestyle opinions that are left behind by everyone who has ever lived. So much of who we are is inherited, but out of that mould we develop our individual journey, whether we've moved far away from our birthplace, our family and its constraints, or remained dutiful to the expectations of a close-knit family. Nothing changes – only the times during which each generation commits itself to the task of changing the world, or to at least stand out and be different from their parents.

By inheriting these illustrations our descendants will be encouraged to follow in the footsteps of our own pioneering spirit. This is no different to our many ancestors who broke boundaries, who were the frontiersmen and women, explorers, pioneers and so on. Even more than that, it's about recognizing that the spiritual journey is one of crossing frontiers and seeking neutrality. After all, we all have ancestors who faced great challenges. We are, by our own nature, nomadic peoples, chosen to explore the many tracks that lead us to a new experience.

The journey that we embark on now, regardless of our age, is spiritual. It marks out the lists of achievements so we can say 'I did my best.' This is what the spiritual journey looks like – to have a vision that nothing is impossible, to recognize when the journey leads us to that point which, symbolically, demands a little more effort to go the extra mile. It's here that you'll find the strength to get you through.

The only hope that humanity can aspire to in years to come is that a generation will be born that has inherited the most ancient wisdoms into which we're all rooted – to realize fully that we're the custodians of the Earth, caretakers of a legacy that began on the First Day. Our actions today will be felt by the next seven generations and this concept is one that encourages us to look ahead beyond ourselves: What do we want to leave for our descendants? What kind of world do we want to bequeath? In these difficult times, it's perhaps our prayers and meditations, our symbolic gestures, that we can at least encourage in our descendants so they might search beyond from the material to the spiritual perspective.

## The spiritual legacy

> *'Even when consciousness is miles away from the ancient conceptions of the rite of renewal, the unconscious still tries to make them accessible to consciousness in dreams.'*
>
> Carl Jung

The descendants in tribal cultures where the elder had the last word create a spiritual legacy for the next generation to continue with those traditions. In Hinduism, the image of Lord Shiva is a semblance of skulls representing cycles of life and death. It symbolizes life that's been lived - for it's the consistency of life and death that augments an opportunity of change, so each generation can improve on the one it leaves behind.

Similarly, the string of prayer beads (*see page 8*) represents our ability to call on an authority greater and wiser than ourselves, each bead being a representation of only a part of the continuum of our ancestry, suggesting this may serve those who believe in a divine principal. We're all connected, whether using the traditional beads of a Buddhist or the devotional Catholic rosary. The skulls of the Hindu God Lord Shiva and the prayer beads of a Buddhist or a Catholic all signify an opportunity for new beginnings. In all their forms, they epitomize salvation and redemption, symbolically representing an unbroken sacred circle. The connection is instilled in each of us, reminding us that what we've lost when a loved one dies is ingrained in the birth of a child. The ancestors enlist their hopes to be realized in the next generation.

The human spirit is proving, as it has done in the past, that even when obstacles are in our way, our intelligence will provide us with the insights to go beyond what can be seen with the naked eye. Whether we choose to look to outer space or journey soulfully to an inner space, it's the legacy that we'll leave behind that's important. Thus we'll encourage our children's children's children never to give up on their own journey, helping them to conquer and overcome fear of the unknown.

We carry the light of our ancestors and, whether we have children ourselves or not, we pass this light to our descendants. In turn, the light is expressed in so many ways, through our creativity, talents, determination, courage, humour and kindness. As we look to our descendants, we can recognize each child carries a different gift or talent. As our ancestors did, we can then nurture them so they, too, can share their gifts with the world.

## The spiritual journey

Once you've learned the importance of practising ancestral healing, the realization or awakening of the knowledge of who you really are begins to make sense. To encourage a spiritual connection, this next exercise can begin that journey by looking towards a road less travelled and one of spiritual connection. To begin is to work with visualization meditations, looking at the spiritual, religious and cultural archetypes you relate to, just as you did with your ancestral stories.

A visualization is a technique to awaken the spirit. Those familiar with this process will recognize the making of the connection with the source into which their spirit is connected, which vibrates on a higher frequency to that of their physical body. If you're not experienced or familiar with this principle, it's highly recommended that before you engage in sacred journeys or visualization adventures, you take some lessons in guided instruction. The nature of your spirit to vibrate to a higher frequency is normal, but learning to reconnect with your physical body is especially important, otherwise you can feel dizzy or unwell when your spirit and physical body merge.

### Visualization

- First, make yourself comfortable, preferably in a seated position or meditative asana (yoga posture).
- Breathe gently, in through the nose and out through the mouth.
- Close your eyes.

- Spend a few moments emptying your mind – a good distraction from thought is to focus on your heartbeat or your breathing.
- When you're ready, visualize yourself in the centre of a circle, awaiting the arrival of your ancestors, both recently deceased and the most ancient.
- At this moment, observe your feet connecting to the Earth as the ground beneath begins to vibrate.
- When you notice your body moving to this vibration, it'll feel like a sacred dance – an awakening inside you.
- Still breathing gently, embrace the ground with the rhythm, as if the earth is opening around you.
- Rising out of the hallowed earth, visualize the ancestors taking their places around you.
- Taking a gentle breath, open your heart to receive their ancient wisdom.
- After a few minutes, or when you feel the power lessening and the vision starts to fade, place your attention back into an easy breathing rhythm.
- Allow your body to recalibrate. Focus on your feet and wiggle your toes, then squeeze your hands into fists.
- When you're ready, open your eyes. Wait until your body has settled before you get up.

By following these steps, you become a gateway or a portal connecting the past to the present. Visualize directing it into the younger generation.

---

## Discovering your legacy – your time to say goodbye

Passing on your legacy to your descendants means teaching them to embrace life's transformative journey through the cycles of life and death. You bequeath to them a material, emotional, cultural and spiritual legacy. One of the ways to pass on a positive legacy is by preparing for your own death. You cannot plan in which way you'll die or when it'll happen, but you can prepare for its eventuality. In many ways, the more prepared you are, the better it is for both you and your legacy.

Just as you might prepare for a birth plan during pregnancy, you should consider preparing a death plan to set out how you'd like to die. For example, you might specify if you want to die at home surrounded by family or in hospital or a hospice. You might create a living will that tells your family how much medical intervention you do or don't want. Do you want to be buried or cremated? What music do you want at your funeral? How do you want to be remembered? All these details help your loved ones to deal with your death in the best possible way. Making a will isn't just a legal exercise – it's a soul one, too. See it as a powerful emotional and psychological journey that can be used to create a space where your family can discuss issues. Preferably air past misunderstandings face to face and listen to each other. Planning is key. While contemplating your death, this is a good time to consider all the other gifts that you give to your descendants, so what they might learn from your life and the choices that you've made can enhance the lives of their own children and so on down the family line.

Fortunately, our own parents were open about their legacy. However, currently in the UK, 70 per cent of people haven't yet written a will and those who have made one rarely discuss it with their family before their death, causing years of misunderstanding and misery for their descendants. Many find talking about death an exceedingly difficult subject to broach, whether this be their own or that of a loved one. But it's important to sort out domestic and financial arrangements and what we want to leave behind for our loved ones.

## Your legacy

The concept of our actions today being felt by the next seven generations is one that should encourage us to look ahead beyond our own personal self-interest and towards protecting the Earth for generations to come. When we can begin to see that we're a link in the evolution chain, we can then see that our lives have the potential to bring change and transformation across time and through many generations to come.

To discover our legacy, sometimes we need to look back at all the stories we've discovered in our journey as ancestral healers. In our profession or work, can we find a connection to something that our father, mother, grandparents and other ancestors attempted to realize from their lifetime?

What's inspired us? What's driven our ambitions? Is there a connection between our life and theirs?

To be able to sanction this ideal is to think about your own legacy and what you'll be passing on to those who come after you. In which areas can our ancestors be our mentors or teachers and help us to be an inspiration for our own descendants? And how do we want to be remembered?

## Establishing your own legacy

Considering the following can help you to become aware of your own legacy:

- What have your children or descendants inherited from their parents and grandparents?
- What aspects of your character do you want your descendants to inherit from you?
- What three words would describe who you are?
- What mistakes would you want your descendants to learn from?
- Name three things that happened that you'd address in a different way now.
- Write down the wisdom that you've learned in your lifetime.
- Make copies – one for yourself and one for your descendants.

---

Give careful consideration to what legacy you wish to leave behind.

# Afterword

In early life, the human ego with all its desires and appetites learns about the social world. It leads us in the choices we make, often leaving our family life and our ancestral connections behind, relegated to being less important until we realize that we couldn't have survived had we not been carried on the shoulders of the ancestors. Furthermore, how would we have found our way had we not been guided by the gifts they've left us?

We learn through knowing that death is but a transition – that to become an ancestor means to have enhanced vision and wisdom so one can be of service to the living. No matter how far away you may be from your homeland or your living family, your ancestors will never fail to support and offer guidance wherever you are. You, too, will be the same for those you love.

*Remember me when I am gone away,*
*Gone far away into the silent land;*
*When you can no more hold me by the hand,*

*Nor I half turn to go yet turning stay.*
*Remember me when no more day by day*
*You tell me of our future that you plann'd:*
*Only remember me; you understand*
*It will be late to counsel then or pray.*
*Yet if you should forget me for a while*
*And afterwards remember, do not grieve:*
*For if the darkness and corruption leave*
*A vestige of the thoughts that once I had,*
*Better by far you should forget and smile*
*Than that you should remember and be sad.*

*Remember*, Christina Rossetti

# References

1. Rash, J., Matsuba, M., Prkachin, K., 'Gratitude and Well-Being: Who Benefits the Most from a Gratitude Intervention?' (*Applied Psychology: Health and Well-Being*, 2011; 3(3)) pp. 350–369
2. McLuhan, T.C., *The Message of Sacred Places: Cathedrals of the Spirit* (Thorsons, 1996) p.146
3. Lawlor, R., *Voices of the First Day: Awakening in the Aboriginal Dreamtime* (USA: Inner Traditions International Ltd, 1991)
4. See www.burkespeerage.com and www.debretts.com
5. Lena and Jose Stevens talk: 'The Three Ancestral Threads and How They Affect Your Present Life', 10 April 2019
6. Berg, P., Singer, M., *George Beadle: An Uncommon Farmer: The Emergence of Genetics in the 20th Century* (NY: Cold Spring Harbor Laboratory Press Books, 2005)
7. Plomin, R., Daniels, D., (2011): 'Children in the same family are very different, but why?' *(Behavioral and Brain Sciences*, Cambridge University Press; 1987; 10(1)) pp.44–59
8. Haque, F.N., Gottesman, I.I., Wong, A.H.C., 'Not really identical: Epigenetic differences in monozygotic twins and implications for twin studies in psychiatry' (*American Journal of Medical Genetics*, Part C, Seminars in Medical Genetics 151C, 2009) pp.136–141
9. Donn, 'the dark one', a Gaelic ancestor

**10.** Rinpoche, S., *The Tibetan Book of Living & Dying* (San Francisco, California: HarperCollins USA, 2013)

**11.** Whistler, L., *The English Festivals* (London: William Heinemann Ltd; 1947)

# Resources

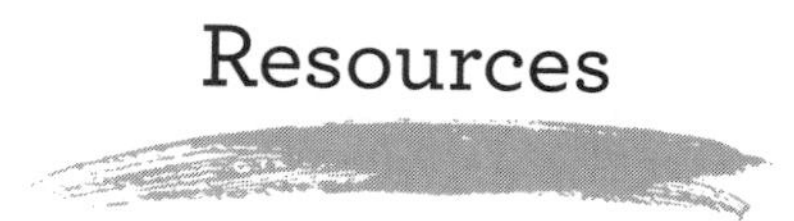

## Books

### *Researching family history*

Bryan Sykes, *The Seven Daughters of Eve* (W.W. Norton & Company, 2002)

Bryan Sykes, *Blood of the Isles* (Corgi, 2007)

Dr Nick Barratt, et al., *Researching Your Family History Online for Dummies* (John Wiley & Sons, Inc., Second Edition, 2009)

George Redmonds, et al., *Surnames, DNA, and Family History* (OUP, Oxford, 2015)

Nancy Hendrickson, *Unofficial Guide to Ancestry.com: How to Find Your Family History on the #1 Genealogy Website* (Family Tree Books, 2nd Ed., 2018)

Juan Pita, *Family Tree Notebook: 7-Generation Genealogy Charts, 127 Ancestor Data Sheets, Tips and Ideas for Further*

*Family Research, Archive and DNA Logs, and a Dedicated Space for Family Stories* (Independently Published, 2020)

Ian Wilson, *Past Lives: Unlocking the Secrets of Our Ancestors* (Seven Dials, 2001)

Anthony Adolph, *Tracing Your Family History* (Collins, 2004)

Megan Smolenyak, *Who Do You Think You Are?: The Essential Guide to Tracing Your Family History* (Viking, 2009)

Mark Herber, *Ancestral Trails: The Complete Guide to British Genealogy and Family History* (Sutton, 2004)

Roger Kershaw, *Migration Records: A Guide for Family Historians* (The National Archives, 2009)

Siddhartha Mukherjee, *The Gene: An Intimate History* (Bodley Head, 2016)

Matt Ridley, *Genome: The Autobiography of a Species in 23 Chapters* (Harper Perennial, 1999)

### Personal histories and self-help

Natalia O'Sullivan and Nicola Graydon, *The Ancestral Continuum: Unlock the Secrets of Who You Really Are* (Simon & Schuster, 2013)

Terry and Natalia O'Sullivan, *Soul Rescuers: A 21st Century Guide to the Spirit World* (Thorsons, 2000)

Anne Ancelin Schutzenberger, *The Ancestor Syndrome: Transgenerational Psychotherapy and the Hidden links in the Family Tree* (Routledge, 1998)

Denise Linn, *Descendants: Tracking the Past... Healing the Future* (Rider Books, 1998)

Denise Linn, *Altars: Bringing Sacred Shrines into Your Everyday Life* (Rider Books, 1998)

Clarissa Pinkola Estés, *Women Who Run with the Wolves: Myths and Stories of the Wild Woman Archetype* (Random House, 1992)

Ivan Cooke, *The Return of Arthur Conan Doyle* (White Eagle Publishing Trust, 1980)

Dr Kenneth McAll, *Healing the Family Tree* (Sheldon, 1997)

Bert Hellinger, et al., *Love's Hidden Symmetry: What Makes Love Work in Relationships* (Zeig, Tucker & Thiesen Inc., 1998)

Mark Wolynn, *It Didn't Start With You: How Inherited Family Trauma Shapes Who We Are and How to End The Cycle* (Viking Books, 2016)

Dr Steven D. Farmer, *Healing Ancestral Karma: Free Yourself from Unhealthy Family Patterns* (Hierophant Publishing, 2014)

David Furlong, *Healing Your Ancestral Patterns: How to Access the Past to Heal the Present* (Atlanta Books, 2014)

Daniel Foor, *Ancestral Medicine: Rituals for Personal and Family Healing* (Bear & Company, 2017)

### *Death and dying*

Felicity Warner, *The Soul Midwives' Handbook: The Holistic & Spiritual Care of the Dying* (Hay House UK, 2013)

Julia Samuel, *Grief Works: Stories of Life, Death and Surviving* (Penguin Life, 2018)

Sogyal Rinpoche, *The Tibetan Book of the Dead* (Thorsons, 1998)

Bill and Judy Guggenheim, *Hello from Heaven: Proof That Life and Love Continue After Death* (Thorsons, 1996)

### *Traditional wisdom*

Robert Lawlor, *Voices of the First Day: Awakening in the Aboriginal Dreamtime* (Inner Traditions International, 1991)

K. Langloh-Parker, *Wise Women of the Dreamtime: Aboriginal Tales of the Ancestral Powers* (Inner Traditions, Bear & Company, 1993)

Malidoma Patrice Somé, *The Healing Wisdom of Africa: Finding Life Purpose Through Nature, Ritual, and Community* (Thorsons, 1999)

Vusamazulu Credo Mutwa, *Song of the Stars: The Lore of a Zulu Shaman* (Barrytown Ltd, 1996)

Vusamazulu Credo Mutwa, *Indaba, My Children: African Tribal History, Legends, Customs and Religious Beliefs* (Payback Press, 1998)

John G. Neihardt, *Black Elk Speaks* (Washington Square Press, 1932)

Dhyani Ywahoo, *Voices of our Ancestors: Cherokee Teachings from the Wisdom Fire* (Shambhala, 1987)

Joseph Campbell and Bill Moyers, *The Power of Myth* (Anchor Books, 1991)

T.C. McLuhan, *The Message of Sacred Places: Cathedrals of the Spiri*t (Thorsons, 1996)

### The aftermath of war

Giles Tremlett, *Ghosts of Spain: Travels Through a Country's Hidden Past* (Faber & Faber, 2008)

Leila Levinson, *Gated Grief: The Daughter of a GI Concentration Camp Liberator Discovers a Legacy of Trauma* (Cable Publishing, 2011)

## Psychotherapy resources

Therapists working in branches developed from the psychodynamic approach often delve into the past. Transpersonal therapists work with a spiritual aspect in their efforts. The BACP and UKCP are the certifying bodies for qualified practitioners. Most should offer a free exploratory phone call to find out if they're the right therapist for you. Family Constellations Therapy also offer individual therapy sessions and group work.

## Websites and resources

### *General information and indexes (free)*

<www.genuki.org.uk> This site provides links to a wide range of genealogical reference sources and websites mainly covering the UK and Ireland.

<www.freebmd.org.uk> Free searchable site of indexes to births, marriages and deaths in England and Wales.

<www.freeukgenealogy.org.uk> Although free, records are limited.

### *Online Records*

<www.ancestry.co.uk> The UK's largest family history site. Also includes records for former British Commonwealth countries.

<www.ancestry.com> This has more emphasis on US and Canadian records, but also has records for the UK, Ireland, Europe, Australia and New Zealand.

<www.familysearch.org> A free site by the Mormon Church (emphasis is on the USA but now has many UK records).

<www.findmypast.co.uk> A fee-paying site to unravel your family history.

<www.myheritage.com> Another paid site that boasts full access to US and UK censuses, in addition to military and immigration records. Once you subscribe, you will also have access to a 'my help' section, where you can speak to or email them for help.

### *Scottish Records*

<www.scotlandspeople.gov.uk> You need to buy credits to access their records and it's the best site of its type. Ancestry also has some digitized Scottish census records.

### *Irish Records*

<http://census.nationalarchives.ie> You can search the 1901 and 1911 censuses for free. Some nineteenth-century records have been destroyed but many sources remain, including census fragments and substitutes covering the years 1821–51.

<https://irelandroots.com> Includes origins of Irish surnames, family trees and some records.

<www.irishorigenes.com> Trace your Irish ancestry through DNA. Also contains information on Irish family names and which parts of Ireland they're from, with links to other Irish family history websites and resources.

Although Irish records between 1821 and 1891 may be problematic, as many of the census records no longer remain, there are other sources such as records of farm estates and manorial records that would include details of who worked there and if they lived on the site.

<www.findmypast.co.uk> This site contains access to Catholic parish registers 1671–1900.

<https://registers.nli.ie> This site contains Catholic parish registers.

# Acknowledgements

A special thank you to our family and friends for their dedication and encouragement so that we could complete this book with the wisdom, grace and compassion that merits its contents and intentions.

All the stories in this book are from our family, friends and clients who allowed us to share their personal narratives and what they've learned from their own ancestral healing. This book couldn't exist without those who enabled us to share their healing journeys. We're profoundly grateful for their generosity and trust in letting us tell their stories.

Our knowledge and understanding of ancestral healing come from addressing and learning about our own ancestral heritage.

We've been immensely fortunate to have met Michelle Pilley, who was at the birth of our writing career with *Soul Rescuers*. It's been both an honour and a delight to have worked with her once more on this book.

To Elaine O'Neill and Emily Arbis, our kind and generous editors who patiently guided us towards the true vision of this book. To the Hay House team for all of their support in the making of this book.

## Further acknowledgements to the contributors

A special thanks to our friends and contributors who have given us their time, advice and generosity on this project. A big thank you to Mira Beattie, who dedicated so much of her time and creativity in supporting us to make sure that the book remained focused on the aims of our writing. And to Lisa Marraffa, who inspired our proposal.

Thank you to our loyal and kind friends Julia Daniels, Philip Jones, Desi Kadra, Carla Santos and Mary Vanderhook for all the extra help with resources, stories and editorial advice.

We've been so fortunate to have been able to call on an international list of fantastic people who have told us about their experiences with their ancestral stories, many of which are being told here for the first time. Those stories are at the heart of this book and even the ones we've been unable to include or acknowledge form part of its life force.

We take full responsibility for any errors or omissions.

We are eternally grateful to Janice Bailey, Olena Baker, Mira Beattie, Maria Bino, Laureen Bishop, Helena Boland, Lisa Bonnice, Jane Burns, Rosamund Burton, Julia Daniels, Anna Font, Atalanta Georgopoulos, Sera Golding, Lucia

Hargasova, Desi Kadra, Ingeborg Hjelt Kamprud, Vos Kels, Louis and Joanna Kovacs, Amanda Lindsay, Jane Maunder, Kay Moseley, Bede O'Sullivan, Araly Padilla, Sarah Jane Pearson, Carla Santos, Kristina Schreitel, Diana Scrimgeour, David Sye, Evelyne Valabregue, Liz Waldron, Rosemary Wanganeen, Angela Watkins, Laura Hayward White, Mark Wolynn.

We're so grateful to our children, Sequoia, Ossian and Bede, who have all made insightful suggestions and lovingly supported us while we've been immersed in this project. We're forever thankful to them all.

To our parents Patrick and Hazel O'Sullivan, and Ferenc and Purita Kovacs Pando, and to all those ancestors before them. To all of the O'Sullivans in the UK and Ireland, the Pando family from Spain, and thank you to our beloved Kovacs family in Hungary.

# About the Authors

Natalia and Terry O'Sullivan met on a spirit rescue workshop that Terry was running as a shaman, teacher and natural-born spiritual medium. He's spent the last 40 years professionally consulting clients and teaching students about the spiritual world. Terry now teaches people how to connect with their spiritual and ancestral attachments, and to harmonize them with both their home and work environment, bringing a new sense of balance to their lives. He has a large healing practice in London and is often invited to work with clients and their families to help heal ancestral and family influences that are causing physical, emotional and psychological problems.

Natalia O'Sullivan is natural healer, psychic and author who has worked in the spiritual and holistic field for over 30 years. She's obtained a mastery of various holistic arts from shamanic traditions and spiritual healing to shiatsu, including soul rescue and ancestral healing, taking on a contemporary approach. Her healing sessions combine ancient knowledge and holistic methods with modern psychological thinking and life-coaching skills to release past negative emotions, in addition to physical and psychological conditions. Her sessions, lectures and workshops adopt a clairvoyant and psychological approach. Natalia's work as an ancestral healer enables the deceased to communicate to help the living with professional choices, relationships, family issues, general health problems, bereavement and psychological disorders such as depression and anxiety.

Together, they co-founded the Soul Rescuers foundation course and Sacred Healer retreats - a professional teaching centre that draws on ancient spiritual traditions. They also developed a training programme for soul rescue practitioners who specialize in sacred and ancestral healing and soul rescue land healing.

For information about Terry and Natalia O'Sullivan's Soul Rescuers workshops, seminars and retreats and to contact the authors regarding their private practice, please email them at **info@soulrescuers.co.uk** or visit their website, **www.soulrescuers.co.uk**.